The French Revolution
By Robert H Wilde

History In An Afternoon 2

History In An Afternoon

Contents

Introduction

The French Revolution was the key event in the formation of modern Europe, the catalyst of vast change which swept the continent, partly through an alteration in people's mindsets and partly, predictably, at the end of a bayonet. A country built piecemeal over centuries was wracked by changes from all aspects of life and led by a man who mishandled just about everything, before the great crucible of history occurred once more: a war, which France did not have to fight, triggering a process of financial turmoil. The deep tensions fractured, the rulers turned to reform to solve the issue and lost control as an emergent ruling class swept the government away, before simultaneously emerging working class threatened to do the same to them. Revolution was exported and the old elites found it impossible to return the world to before.

That's not all the French Revolution was.

The French Revolution is also the world's greatest example of a positive, well-meaning event going terribly wrong. It begs the question: how did France sweep away a centuries' old 'feudal' system in just a few remarkable days? And how did they go from being inspired by liberty, personal freedom and individual rights to a government which ruled through terror only a few years later? I mean Terror with a capital T, a deliberate policy of fear and execution which pursued an idea of purity like a B-movie villain made real. How did leaders who wanted a democratic state change into people waging a 'holocaust for liberty', as contemporary Fabre d'Églantine called for?

Plenty of answers to this have been forwarded, usually to bolster an ideological point, such as the collapse into brutality being the inevitable endpoint of Enlightenment thought (forwarded by conservatives opposed to Enlightened ideas). The history of the French Revolution isn't just the story of how the modern European world formed, although it's a fascinating tale filled with as many set pieces as any fiction. It's also the analysis of what's in all of us, of human nature and how it reacts to pressure and change. This book will argue that no stage of the revolution was pushed along by a single cause; rather that it was a large interplay of factors. It will also argue that the leader in this pack was human nature, in all its various, chaotic and irrational forms, not ideology or the power of some quasi-mystical force like liberty or capital.

I've said 'stage' of the revolution, because the events went through several. I don't just mean things like Monarchy, Terror, Directory. I mean clear but much more subtle beginnings. The revolution wasn't one action and a reaction, it was a series of constant changes. You start with a financial crisis, and you go through a number of stages in which what's happening fundamentally changes before you even get a whiff of a guillotine. The people rebelling in declaring a National Assembly are doing something different to when they cancel 'privilege' a short time later. We will examine all these.

The French Revolution has produced iconic images, but tricolours and slogans like 'Liberty, Equality and Fraternity' are second to the guillotine, a method of execution perfected to bring equality to murder, a strange line of thought we will see increasingly more of as the revolution develops. Indeed, from the judgement of historians to the tone of major cultural works, there's been a battle over whether the revolution was good or bad. That's an outdated binary concept we used to call Manichean and humanity is perfectly capable of mixing good and bad elements, as the Revolution did. This book aims to present a complex event better considered a living organism, rather than judge it by the standards of now, or even then.

It's easy to pinpoint the start date of the Revolution and that's the events of 1788/9: the French king tried to dredge up a relic of the past to rubber-stamp tax, and this relic didn't just bite the hand that (didn't) feed them, it tore down the whole government and put itself in control. Bringing a representative body called the Estates General back from the dead was already desperation, but it was so old no one really knew how to structure it. Into this gap of uncertainty rushed a generation of people high on dreams of liberty. It's harder to decide where to start a book because you need context, and I've gone back to two different wars, one a different revolution; that of the American Colonies. The American Revolution was deeply affected by French involvement, just as the French Revolution was in a large part triggered by the same.

What's entirely uncertain is where the revolution ended. Some historians bring their accounts to an end after the fall of the Terrorists and Thermidor, the end of what might be called the 'mob phase'. Others continue through the Directory to the rise of the Napoleonic empire, sensing a change here and suggesting—sometimes only by accidental implication—that Bonaparte actually 'ended' what had gone before by cunning design. In recent years there has been a trend for textbooks to continue to the fall of Napoleon and the return of a king. This book will end when Napoleon made himself emperor, and explain how this was only possible because he brought closure to the immediate events of the revolution.

Many later revolutions would look to the French for examples of how to act, or for warnings of what not to do. Even the Russian Revolution a century later would operate under the spectre of what had occurred in France and the Bolsheviks would explicitly consider themselves Russian 'Jacobins' who needed to create their own Terror. You don't need to know anything about either era to know that was a very bad thing— the last word is enough. However, the French Revolution did not have this hindsight. For right or wrong, the revolutionaries of 1789 felt they were out on their own in a new world with no history to learn from. They looked to ancient Rome, but the certainty of traditions and experience was gone, with answers having to be created to problem after problem. The tapestry of France fell apart when the warp threads were pulled out and the revolutionaries had to knit a replacement after making their own needles. It went wrong—of course it did—there was panic, fear and paranoia. That's why it went wrong.

This narrative history explains what happened during the French Revolution, and gives a grounding should you wish to go on into—often fierce—debates. It's for both students and interested general readers, so there's a crib sheet at the end of each chapter.

The aim of this book, and this series, is to allow readers to enjoy learning about the essentials of a historical event in a long afternoon. I love huge, detailed, often dry history books; this series is for people who don't. The subject might, and sometimes must, be serious, but the explanation can be enjoyable.

1: Winning The Revolution (But Not That Revolution)

You can always find someone who said "I told you so". The key thing to remember about history and hindsight is: to that monarch or president etc., it wasn't so clear. In this chapter the honour of being right goes to Anne Robert Jacques Turgot, who told French king Louis XVI in 1774 that financial restraint was vital else "the first gunshot will drive the state to bankruptcy". Sadly, historians don't have to pluck Turgot from obscurity to find that quote, as he was Comptroller General of Finances, a position that doesn't need much translating. In 1774 Turgot had been appointed as head of the French government's accounts and he doubled down on his initial assessment in 1776, when he tried but failed to convince his king that a war would destroy the monarchy's finances and cause their enemies no real harm at all. He was to be proved right, but he was one voice in a French government who included many advocates of war, not least of which was the voice in Louis XVI's head.

You may be wondering, what war? It became known as both The American Revolutionary War and the American War of Independence and started as a conflict between Britain and the American colonists they ruled. Why was Louis interested? The answer to that lies with the past. There were two major historical pressures forcing Louis XVI down the route he took in the 1770s, and they were Louis XIV and the Seven Years' War.

The Sun King

Louis XIV reigned France for seventy-two years, long enough for a whole generation of his countrymen to know no other ruler. After suffering a civil war as a youth, Louis took power and involved himself in all aspects of his kingdom, inspiring an artistic movement which secured France as the cultural leader in Europe, and a political approach which came the closest Europe ever saw to true Absolute Monarchy. Louis took power from his nobles and wrapped the country around his control by using a vast palace at Versailles as a geographic heart of the nation. He fought a series of wars in which he just came out on the right side and earned the name the Sun King. Although we now question his achievements—his challenge to religious tolerance chief among the issues—he is still regarded as the greatest monarch of his age.

As you can imagine, this made Louis XIV a very hard act to follow. It wasn't just that Louis had a long list of successes, including a relatively prodigious life, but that the system he had created could only be run by a genius like him. Much like Bismarck later, Louis had ridden through waves of assaults that his successors simply weren't equipped for. His successor, great-grandson Louis XV in 1715, looked pale in comparison.

The First World War

Louis XV was five when he came to power, and he would rule until 1774. A long rule, a long life, but as it followed the Sun King it was still overshadowed. This Louis continued to do what French monarchs always did—fight against, and alongside, a varying combination of the 'Great Powers' Austria, Britain, Prussia, and Russia. He managed to gain the Ducky of Lorraine for France even while losing the 'succession' part of the War of the Polish Succession, and he conquered the Austrian Netherlands, which was then given back to Austria. Given that the French people regarded Austria as their ferocious enemy, Louis' reputation in France suffered, and hold that thought because in a minute there's a marriage with Austria which helps this all spiral into disaster.

The real problem with Louis XV, however, was that he lost the first world war. Not, as you might have suddenly thought, the First World War of 1914 to 1918, but the first truly global conflict which is better known by several other names, chiefly The Seven Years' War (1756 – 63). In Europe, this conflict was dominated by Frederick the Great of Prussia, a titan of the age. Here, France fought in alliance with Austria, Russia, Sweden and others against Prussia, Hanover and Britain. Frederick survived the war by one of the most fortuitous moments in history, namely the Russian ruler dying and being replaced by someone who made peace. After several years of conflict, no one in Europe had managed to win a decisive victory, and the increasingly exhausted nations looked at their empty coffers and came to peace.

France had focused on Europe first, and Frederick. Britain's forces, however, had done the opposite. They sent few troops to the mainland and decided instead to mount a war of imperial conquest against the global possessions of France and Spain. Britain had the better navy, they took the initiative and a worldwide war took place. Britain conquered French trading posts in Africa, rich regions of the West Indies, threw France out of India and seized the hub of Spain's Caribbean network. France lost the global battle and they sat down to peace discussions having been humiliated.

But that isn't all. In the USA, the Seven Years' War has a different name which relates to their local struggle. The French-Indian War was a conflict between France and Britain, their respective colonists and Native American allies. Britain started the war ruling the 'Thirteen Colonies', while France was just as original with 'New France'. The border between the two had seen several wars and the tensions in America had helped start Britain and France fighting each other on Frederick's playground. Britain initially did badly, but soon adapted and UK Prime Minister Pitt gave the British colonists ever more autonomy while changing the military to fight in the terrain.

One of the colonial soldiers who fought in this conflict was called George Washington, later first President of the independent USA. By 1760, the French-Indian war was all but over, and peace had to wait for Europe to catch up. As France and Britain stood at the negotiating table, the former had to give the latter all North American territory east of Mississippi, including Canada. There were other changes, but you get the picture: the Seven Years' War ended and France hadn't just been embarrassed in Europe, it had been made a laughing stock around the world.

France wanted revenge. The army, the people, the monarch—they thirsted for a chance to take the war to Britain once more and gain everything back. Louis XVI came to power in the shadow of one of the continent's greatest rulers and a military defeat he was expected to avenge. The pressure was on.

Louis XVI: Man and King

Louis XVI wasn't a man well suited to pressure. He was the third son of the heir to the French throne, and in 1774 he inherited the crown aged 19. He wasn't, as some accounts claim, a stupid man, but he was too interested in small details to notice bigger pictures, had been taught to be aloof from the everyday Frenchman, was reserved, and his genuine interest in the state of his country was not backed by the force of will or personality to change it. Sadly, Louis XVI provides us with his own perfect summary: he loved English history and was determined to learn from the mistakes of English king Charles I, who was beheaded in a revolution. I think we can conclude those lessons were not learned.

Louis had another problem, and that was Marie Antoinette. The pair had married in 1770 and entered into a whole world of difficulty because Marie was an Austrian archduchess and daughter of the Holy Roman Empress Marie Theresa. There were some very good reasons why the ruler of France might want to cement an alliance with those states, but the people of France considered Austria a rival, and from the very beginning Marie was considered an enemy by many on the street and suffered printed slurs so offensive the modern press would be jealous. When Marie didn't immediately produce any heirs she was further lambasted, although the lack of children was entirely a psychological issue with Louis.

Louis could not shake the fear that Marie had been sent by Austria to coerce him into acting their way, and he feared letting Marie have too much control. It's worth mentioning that this was exactly why Marie's family had married her to him, and why most other political marriages occurred throughout time, but you weren't supposed to be paranoid about it.

Louis then began to rule France, and his actions unravelled those of his predecessors. France had a tier of government called the 'parlements', which was a gathering of dozens of judges. Louis XV had spent years trying to reduce their power, but Louis XVI restored them, partly because he allowed himself to be persuaded by a court faction, but also for his wonderfully foreshadowing belief that it was what the people of France wanted. A swell of public support followed, but restoring the parlements meant they were now a friction on the use of royal power once more. Why did Louis restore the parlements? He believed he was a reforming monarch who listened to the people, whoever they were. But this image was just that, a picture, and he took no lead in reforms, preferring to allow ministers to attempt things, then failed to back them adequately. His government broke down into factions desperate for support.

Louis undermined the work of Louis XIV, because his social failings meant he didn't like interacting with nobles and he began to ignore court. Where XIV had wrapped the nobility around him at Versailles, XVI let it decay and they drifted away. Furthermore, Louis was a powerful man in the sense people weren't easily allowed to correct him, and he was able to develop silence as a tool: if he didn't want to argue (which he rarely did), if he disagreed, he would just stay silent to questions or policy.

The American War of Independence

The French-Indian War / Seven Years' War left Britain in charge of large areas of North America, but that victory had complications which would never be settled before they exploded into a new war. The flash point was not Britain versus France, it was the relationship of Britain to the colonists. War had pressurised this, and war twists and breaks. The common narrative of the American War of Independence is that Britain tried to tax the colonists without giving them a voice, and No Taxation without Representation led to a rebellion, a war and the British yoke being thrown off.

There is another way of looking at it. As I will also stress about the king and people of France, the relationship between Britain and the colonies was pressured in many ways, including colonist demands to expand westwards. Britain had, in one way, defended the colonists from France in the war and that had cost Britain money. They had spent a great deal on troops to fight the war, and were still spending money after to garrison the area. The colonists chaffed under British rule but Britain was paying to defend them from French attacks and revenge. When Britain tried to expand tax coverage of the colonies, it wasn't being a grasping imperial monster, it was trying to recoup costs. You can argue No Taxation without Representation, but you can also argue Payment for Services Rendered.

Either way, a rebellion began in 1774 and the colonists divided, a third supporting Britain, a third the rebellion and a third remaining neutral. A war for the colonies was now fought in the colonies. Britain had a huge supply line and a series of questionable commanders, while the colonists had Seven Years' War veterans who'd already mastered the style needed to fight successfully. Britain had the old attitudes of the past, while Congress had the dreams of the present; we will explore these in more depth during the French Revolution.

You can imagine why the French viewed this war with such interest. Britain was distracted, growing weaker in their other commitments as more troops and money went to America. Furthermore, France now had a ready-made reason and invitation to get involved in a war, because pretending to have the moral high ground was still important. People in France agitated to help the colonists throw off Britain's greedy hands, even though the colonists were rejecting a system of government more liberal than that of their own. Turgot warned against involvement, but others pushed for it. Foreign Secretary Vergennes declared "Providence had marked this moment out for the humiliation of England," and of course, if this book was written in 1785, it would be him opening this chapter telling us so. France also had the chance for a different war, as France's queen was closely related to the Austrian emperor, and he wanted support fighting Prussia. Louis didn't want to fight two wars at once again (so one lesson of the Seven Years' War had been learned), and he decided to bloody England's nose rather than support his in-laws.

At first the help was secretive, but after the British had to surrender an army at Saratoga, France publicly declared a commitment to the colonists ... except their plan to do this involved attacking British targets around the globe. The war for the colonies was turned into a world war between two imperial powers.

This isn't overstating it. Britain considered quitting the colonies instantly to fight fully against France and eyed the West Indies as a suitable replacement for the rebellious American lands. With their intentions in America changing, with their eye on the world, British forces continued the American War of Independence at half-mast for several years. An attempt to take the South went wrong, and a combined Franco-American army under Washington and Rochambeau forced British commander Cornwallis and his army to surrender.

The British decided to surrender to the colonists, but not *because* of the colonists. Again and again, British history would be marked by initial failures in war followed by a redoubling of effort and victory: pushed back in the Napoleonic War, pushed back in World War One, pushed off the mainland in World War Two. But in America, Britain didn't redouble because they didn't want to fight the world war which by then included France, Holland and Spain against them, with battles being fought in the Mediterranean, West Indies, West Africa and

India. Britain stepped back bloody and embarrassed but still keeping a lot of their global territory. The USA was created, and France celebrated their revenge.

Except ... who really won and lost? American patriots won, of course, although they would need a civil war for their rhetoric to become reality. But France didn't have to get involved in this war, didn't have to spend all the money (over a billion livres, when royal income was very much not measured in that many zeroes), and you will see how that turns into Louis XVI being overthrown and executed. The British didn't have to fight it and they didn't let it destroy them; they stepped back and their king was fine, their economy managed, and they were in a position to fund the war against Napoleon. The pressures they faced in terms of power moving from upper to middle class (a theme we will return to in France) were not cooked until they turned violent. Louis XVI lost the American War of Independence in the long term far more than British / Britain's equivalents ever did. A British prime minister resigned, the French king was executed. Britain lost land in America, but France would have to sell theirs at a huge discount soon enough anyway. This was not a decision of grand currents and powerful impersonal forces. France did not have to fight. It was a decision taken by the king and his ministers. Turgot was right. The rest of this book will explain how and why.

CRIB

- France, considered one of the great world powers, is beaten in the Seven Years' War by Britain and loses territory and considerable pride.
- The new French monarch, Louis XVI, is expected to restore this lost pride, but is a socially awkward man who can't lead.
- In search of revenge, France enters into the American War of Independence on the colonists' side and helps them beat Britain.
- Unfortunately, the considerable costs of this war were funded through loans, leaving the French throne in perilous financial trouble.

2: Cracks: France Before the Revolution

Louis XVI became King of France on May 10th, 1774. But what was France? That's not some philosophical question because while there had, for centuries, been a throne which ruled a kingdom called France, that was as homogenous as it got. The Holy Roman Empire gets all the grief about being a splintered mess, but there wasn't one 'France' once you got below the very highest levels. The crown which Louis inherited had been expanding for centuries, not just in terms of geography but in terms of rights and laws and culture. As the heartland of this kingdom had grown and grown, so the French monarchs had collected more and more former states and these were rarely reformatted to match the unit they joined. Instead things had been adapted, from necessity, to keep it all going. Every layer of interaction between the different aspects of France caused friction. Even language varied by locality and class to the point people meeting from across France might not understand each other. France was a badly cut jigsaw puzzle ready to be knocked off the table. Friction causes fires, and that happened in 1789.

Vast Variation

By 1789 there would be twenty-eight million people in France (a nearly 50% increase in just eighty years), and they lived in a country divided into provinces which varied in size from huge

Britany to tiny Flanders. Except, they also lived in a country divided into 'generalities' and the borders didn't match. Also, there were thirty-nine government positions called Provincial Governors but they were window dressing, and thirty-six Intendants of 'generalities' with practical administrative roles and a much more even distribution, and the two clashed. But don't forget the parlements, thirteen courts / sources of local representation which further divided the country into thirteen regions, the biggest being the Parlement of Paris, which covered a full third of continental France and annoyed everyone in equal ratio. The church divided France into its own patterns, and they all chaffed because the boundaries were indistinct. True, the generalities were a relatively recent creation which didn't often overlap, but the parlements and provinces could spend days arguing over lines on a map and who was responsible for what. If you had a legal dispute in France, from a tax issue to wanting a building permit, finding who was meant to solve it was not easy.

And as if that wasn't complicated enough, there wasn't just one legal system overseeing all of this, let alone one with clear borders. Everything had been adapted as it had been added, so things like tax and marriage—in fact, every form of official interaction between people—varied depending on where you were in the kingdom. It wasn't just paperwork, as differing weights and measures could be found in different regions. You can imagine what the state of different languages was. If you stayed in your village your whole life this might be manageable, but any broader interaction brought cost, conflict and recourse to higher authorities who would then argue too. Then again, if you bought anything coming into your village from elsewhere you'd suffer due to the excess of local tolls and taxes.

The early sections of this book will talk a lot of complaints over tax, so let's focus on some. France had a major tax called the 'taille'—in fact, it was *the* main direct tax. But in some parts of France it was assessed per person, and in others by the amount of land owned, and that's a pretty staggering difference to modern readers. Meanwhile the 'gabelle' was a salt tax which had multiple levels depending on where you were, one of which was paying nothing at all because of a historical exemption. In short, anyone with the slightest bit of knowledge about the French kingdom could become very annoyed about their (mis)treatment and human interactions could disappear into knots like an early modern Kafka. This tangle of human interactions was added to a richly diverse physical environment.

Paris had always been the heart of the French kingdom, even when there hadn't been enough power to warrant the name, and it was the most homogenous region with a huge power base. Decisions taken in Paris could spread out through this Paris basin quickly and efficiently, and that way they would have the weight and strength to be carried to the many chaffing provinces. What we'll see in this book is how the revolution started and took firm hold of the Paris region, and encountered all sorts of interactions (including civil war) when it went into the edges.

There were further divisions. France was officially Catholic with pockets of fierce Protestantism carefully tolerated because there was no easy way to rid themselves of it.

An Out of Date State

The divisions we have seen above weren't universally unpopular, because they could be exploited. The crown in particular had spent generations sliding through the gaps in the system and bending things to its will. However, the state was not strong. It too was riven with issues. France had grown in an ad hoc manner, and the systems of royal and government power generally had too. No one had wiped the slate clean and installed a modern system designed to cope with the issues of the 1780s. Instead, Louis XVI found himself ruling a state that had developed over the medieval period and last been heavily modified during the internal and external conflicts of the early Bourbons. The Sun King had wrapped the state around him, Cardinal Richelieu had precursored him, but each iteration of state had formed in reaction to what was needed in that era. Louis XIV only just held his grand design together enough to fight a series of great wars. In this era, Europe was ever-changing, and warfare—to pick out one element—required more money, men and resources than ever before. Louis XVI had to take part in the American Revolutionary War with a system designed to fight battles generations earlier—not meaning the types of weapons, but the funding of them. Louis XVI had an early modern (and often medieval) government but modern issues, and his vast debts were caused by the deficiencies in the French crown to deal with that new world. France didn't have a modern bureaucracy, but it needed one. There was always going to need to be reform as the world evolved, and Louis XVI faced his need like XIV had done. The result would be very different. Chief among the frictions caused by an out of date state was the fact that tax revenue hadn't expanded to meet expenditure, chiefly from wars. There were always a lot of these now that Europe had both new nations competing to dominate like Prussia, and the old nations had turned into colonial powers with land all over the globe to defend. People tried reforms, people knew crown income needed to be larger, but the tangled mass of France's very building blocks made such change incredibly hard.

You might be thinking that the French crown had levied a large set of taxes, which is to say the average people of France were already paying a lot and the crown wanted more. Economic studies have, in fact, revealed that the average Briton was paying twice as much in tax as a Frenchman. So it wasn't that France was overtaxed, it was that the poor French state and web of tensions meant only a limited amount could be got at, and the taxation was spread unequally. The citizens of Paris were the most taxed people in Europe, in a country where some nobles paid basically nothing. There was no easy way to reform the system to get more and or get it fairly.

In theory, Louis XVI had vast power, but the committees of state officials between him were riven with faction and infighting, and the whole fractured mess of France was reflected in the divisions of the highest state officials in the land, who bickered among each other to wrest the most power from the king.

Agriculture and Inheritance

The agricultural sector of France famously had two things wrong with it, at least if you judged from the ivory tower of thriving neighbours. Firstly, it had learned little from the agricultural revolution which had begun in Britain. Of course, as you've seen, you can't easily generalise in France and some areas *were* improving. For example, the region around Paris was gaining from economies of scale and industrialised agricultural methods. But overall, French agriculture was still an inefficient producer leaving every peasant (and urban resident) afraid of famines and leading to regular periods of starvation. Farmers stood a better chance of eating because they could take their supplies first, but the residents of Paris and other urban areas dreaded bread shortages. But hold that thought.

Perhaps the most famous problem in all of pre-revolutionary France was the inheritance issue. Vast swathes of the nation passed land from parents to children by dividing it equally between the latter, and several centuries of this left much of France divided into very small units unable to use economies of scale. Eighty per cent of France was rural peasantry wrapped up in customs, laws, dues and payments, such as where cattle could be grazed and whose job it was to clear the roads of fallen trees. The church had no such problem with its land, which stayed intact.

The agricultural situation produced two fault lines. During the years of Louis XVI, the weather and crop difficulties led to an increasing number of bad harvests, which led to many people going hungry. There were issues with crops in fields, with wine, with animals... The period became one of great uncertainty over food. Since agriculture was the biggest industry, it's easy to say that was a major source of friction, but the truth is much starker: everyone needs to eat, and often they couldn't. In the decades before 1789 the standard of living for peasants was actually falling.

When you can't eat, hunger turns to anger. So where was it directed? Partly by urban residents at farmers, partly by everyone at the government. The peasants of France were emerging snail-like from a system we once called feudal. The landlords of France had been able, in many different ways in different places, to exact pretty much any demand you could think of, from proportions of your harvest to a noble in Toulouse who, thanks to some bizarre quirk of history, could levy a tax every time he bought land for himself. And while the late eighteenth century had seen large changes from the landlord favouring medieval extreme, your average peasant could still argue with landlords, current and old, over money and goods which the latter couldn't easily afford to hand over. So many people grew angry at the elites over them, and the systems of government which were linked to them. Peasants could first be angry at the well-off among them who owned land, hired the rest and lived with profit—the French kulaks. But there didn't have to be failed crops for tension to rise. If producers weren't confident they wouldn't profit, they wouldn't spend their excess on industrial products. Urban areas, and the people in them, felt vulnerable. A whole class of awakening urban minds wondered how this was happening and whether it could be stopped. When tensions were aflame, the French peasant (and, in many examples, urban residents) could swing into action in one of the many food riots which burn in history.

A lot of this book is going to focus on the actions of the middle class and the major role they played. But what you'll find in this book is how much the bourgeoise's actions were actually a reaction to those of the peasants, and that's a trend that often gets ignored. The peasants, in the 1770s and 1780s, were growing just as frustrated with the status quo as anyone else, and we see evidence for this in the growing quantity of legal challenges aimed at the landowners, as well as the violent challenges in riots and attacks. Of course, the vast majority of France's population consisted of peasantry but there was variation in the status of peasants. This wasn't just poor peasants angry at capitalist landowners in a Marxist cliché, because the seigneurial rights and dues that landowners still had in 1789 boggle the modern mind. For instance, in some parts of France peasants were obliged to only use the lord's mills to grind corn with an associated charge, creating / sparking a perfect storm of anger over food and dues. A vast amount of peasant life, even for those who owned land, was tied to a higher social class. Of course the state was at the top of this pyramid, with their taxes, and the peasants rebelled against this even more. The complaints of the peasants in the late 1780s are filled with anger at this friction. That in 1789 and beyond the peasants often attacked the landowners was not new. The scale and reaction was just different.

The Towns

The growing sense of social awareness among the educated of the cities wasn't driven purely by empathy and morality. It was often driven by fear. The cities had a growing population density, poor sanitation, high death rates and a large number of visible poor. In fact, France saw a stark contrast between the wealthy elites and those in poverty, which, defined as people without adequate income to support them, numbered between eight and ten million in a population of less than thirty million. Poverty didn't behave differently in pre-revolutionary France to elsewhere: it hit those unable to work hardest, such as the old and the ill, and tended to cause greatest concern when the able-bodied men found themselves sunk into it. Poverty begat crime, which scared the haves, and begging, which was visible to the haves, as well as prostitution, which the haves exploited. The poverty of France provided a class of people with no attachment to the status quo (the poor) and a class of people who felt the status quo could be changed to solve the awful problem (the scared and the kind).

The rural poor tended to move to the towns, where the high death rates kept a turnover of people going. At any one time, twenty per cent of France's population was in the towns. Even here, however, the poor had little hope for advancement up a social ladder. Skills, crafts and education were fiercely protected, with guilds acting as a control for anyone hoping to work in anything other than the dangerous, carrying-things end of industry, so the poor stayed in poverty as they worked thankless jobs that frequently threw them on the mercy of alms houses and charities. The annoyed wondered why the guilds should have such control, and why the government was fat and they were dependant on private handouts.

The symbol of 'old regime' control in industry is the livret. In 1776, guilds came under fire and it looked like they might be abolished. However, not only were the guilds allowed to return but a few years later every worker had to carry a livret, a passport-like document which employers had to sign if they agreed people could leave. Urban workers felt controlled in good times, abandoned in bad ones, and on the cusp of poverty if not actually in it.

The most common call was not for a wage increase to counter the inflation-led collapse in the value of money, or for a reduction in taxes, but for the state to put controls in place to limit food prices so people could still earn and buy produce. Food shortages were felt most acutely in the towns because peasants tended to take their own food in the country, and these shortages were when the threads of civilisation most frayed, when fights and riots and thefts occurred at their most intense. The rioting part of that is easily understood in today's world— we have rioting—but the price controls are less easy. Many government officials were tasked with monitoring the price of food and acting to keep it down if needed, especially in Paris where the defence of the realm was believed to be linked to keeping the capital away from rioting and, dare we even say, revolution. People wouldn't just steal food, they would assault people charging too much or accused of hoarding food to benefit from higher prices, and the mob would sell any supplies they found at what they considered a fair value. The French Revolution wasn't the first time a mob of disaffected urbanites would use violence to effect a change, it was just on a much, much grander scale, and these mobs weren't purely those in poverty but those about to be reduced to it, i.e. pretty much everyone.

A New Middle Class

But only pretty much, because there was a secure elite. To be fair, there were three secure elites, with the by-definition elite being the nobility, which along with the clergy numbered in the low hundreds of thousands. By far the biggest category of the well-off was the middle class, the bourgeoisie, who by the time of the revolution numbered around two million.

That statistic needs some very important clarifying. Firstly, that's two million people in a country nearing thirty million, so this middle class was a small percentage, but they had attached to them some staggering figures. The middle class owned a quarter of the land and a large amount of the wealth. Any fortune that was made, any modest comfort that was attained, was generally sunk into land, be it an old estate or a house in a city with new walls. That was for the adults, while the children would be educated to a better standard and have an office bought for them.

Furthermore, the middle classes were growing, and at speed. While the general population of France added lower percentages, the middle class doubled in size between the vastly successful Louis XIV and the vastly disastrous Louis XVI. It is fair to say that the latter had to deal with a middle class of growing power, presence and awareness that no previous French king needed to. By Louis XVI's reign, the situation in France had changed. The middle class were also developing their own culture. This had taken a while because the most successful of them bought themselves promotion to the nobility, so the cream kept being skimmed off. But they were prey to the same desire to display wealth that every elite showed the world over, and they invested in new buildings, art forms, and produce. They also invested in newspapers and pamphlets, libraries and encyclopaedias. The French middle class were aware, keen readers and thinkers. Along with middle class status came a huge number of benefits and privileges which varied across the country with no consistency. Of course, there was no one face to this culture: it was as multi-faceted as any other aspect of France. But there was a growing consciousness of public affairs and being a part of public opinion. The bourgeois hydra was waking. Yes, successful bourgeoisie could enter the nobility via purchase, but as we will see below, that was a whole new world of friction.

Venal Offices: Buying Your Job and Government

We now come to a concept mostly missing from modern Western society, but which will be very important in the first few days of the revolution: venal offices. These were government positions, such as a post in the judiciary, military or government, but they weren't given out based on ability. No, venal offices were purchased by people with the money who wanted the esteem and income they provided. They started in the 1500s as a way of the crown raising money, and by 1789 there was a brisk trade, because once you bought the office you kept it by paying an annual tax. You could pass it on (say to children), or sell it (to the highest bidder) as you pleased.

By 1789 the venal office was going through a crisis. Over seventy thousand were in existence, covering huge areas of life (such as almost the entire legal system). However, despite that number, demand was great as the middle class expanded and the prices soared. Venal offices were experiencing a powerful inflation / market bubble, creating plenty of annoyed prospective customers who wanted to buy into the hierarchy.

Nobility

There was a crossover between the middle and upper classes, partly when it came to bourgeoisie who could afford to just live off their land. Over four thousand venal offices actually made you into an official noble, and thousands of middle-class buyers were able to seize these highly demanded positions and upgrade themselves. Having done so, they were looked down upon by the historical nobility (who tried to stop people buying in) and hated by the middle class they'd left behind.

Before 1789 being a noble was still a highly desirable goal. The nobles carried with them the weight of tradition and the sense of age-old power and glory. Society saw the nobility as their own 'order', with their coats of arms, special courts and the ultimate final thumbing of the nose: you could be decapitated with a sword instead of hanged, although it would be fair to say no one actually wanted to invoke that right. Of more practical concern was the sheer amount of rights, ranks and privileges they had. We've met the gabelle, the salt tax: nobles were largely exempt. You've also met the taille: they were entirely exempt. These were the badges of nobility that everyone knew, more powerful symbols to the commoners than any waist worn sword. Nobility comprised the court, the intendents, most of the military officers, all but one of the Ministers, and most of the upper clergy.

I said earlier the nobles numbered in the low hundreds of thousands, and that's because there is no exact figure. A quarter of a million nobles is in the middle of the best estimates, and they held a quarter of the land in France, a quarter of the revenue from the Church, and all the highest venal offices. The king tended to only involve himself with nobles, and almost the entire top-level government of France, from king's counsellors to army commanders, were noble. The rare occasions when non-nobles worked at the top of France's political system were shockingly unusual.

But ... there is a big 'but'. As old noble families lost money, so the newly rich bought their way into the nobility and kept it the top of the tier, the true elite of France. There were plenty of 'poor' nobles, if we define that as people with noble rank but wealth no higher than your average bourgeoisie, perhaps more than half of them all being less than this, but there were very few wealthy people who weren't noble. Rising stars of the middle class could invest in a venal office, or the hand of a poor but noble heiress. The result was a system which drew wealth close to the top of France but left these classes riven with anger and friction. The most successful of the lower orders rose to become nobles, refreshing their class, but old nobility warred with new nobility. A law passed in 1781 said to be an army officer you had to come from four generations of nobility. What you won't see in this book in 1789 is a class war of middle versus upper class. What you will see is the middle class, and a large chunk of the nobility, taking on the political leaders and structures of France.

In a sense, reform of the state was incredibly difficult because of the opposition of noble families who had so much invested in it, and who could cause problems. That doesn't mean the threat of nobles retreating to their estates and gathering troops. As Louis XIV had pulled the nobility tightly into court, it meant factions of nobles playing internal politics rather than looking at what was needed. People opposed Turgot, Necker and others not simply because they disagreed with the reforms (although they did), but because they were from a different court faction. The government of France was divided into a set of school-like cliques and no one managed to gain a secure enough hold to carry through reforms. They would have, had the king been stronger and listened to who he'd appointed, but Louis XVI was a toy boat on a river being pulled about by currents.

The Clergy

The nobles were actually the 'second order' of France's three, commoners being ranked only third. The first order were the clergy, who accounted for around 130,000 of the population. They were highly unevenly distributed—a small number given the Church held a tenth of France's land—and these clergy were entitled to a tithe of a tenth of everyone's income (not including those oh so diverse privileges) and they didn't pay the same tax as everyone else. That was partly due to the clergy having their own General Assembly which met regularly and repelled the interests of royal finance. In a way, the clergy were ahead when it came to people who knew how to form their own committee in 1789. That said, the clergy also knew how to leverage the monarch's needs, and they agreed gifts in return for privileges. With their huge landholdings, the Church could borrow large sums easily, which could be given to the king and paid off through Church income. This left the monarch indebted to the Church and less likely to interfere. It was a cunning gift-and-debt system.

Only Catholicism was official, and most education and 'poor relief' came from its organisation. However, the friction here wasn't commoners looking at this elite group of rich and powerful. The truth was, most clergy were neither rich nor powerful. All the same forces of unequal wealth distribution, climbing the ranks through family finances and noble domination affected the clergy just as they did secular society. Your average village priest was a vitally important source of information and moral nourishment to his congregation, but he was likely less well off (he had enough money behind him to complete the course of study), while the highest ranks of the Church were held by nobles who drew huge incomes and who had done what those at the bottom might consider 'abuse of the system' to get there. By the 1780s, the lower ranks of the

Church were engaged in campaigns to reform the top ranks, while the upper class were finding ways to stamp down the lower.

Visible Despotism aka Louis XV Conjures the Estates General Dream

We met the parlements of France earlier. The legal system in of France required all new laws to be passed through them, meaning they could, if they so desired, attempt to frustrate the process of government and act as a form of opposition. Several factors weighed against this, but the main was one the *lit de justice*. This was the process in which the king arrived at the parlement and dictated in person the new law, and it was absolutely impossible to stop unless you happened to have an army wanting a civil war. Parlements could oppose the king to make a point, moan a lot when he turned up, but ultimately they did exactly what he said because they didn't want civil disobedience or even bloodshed. The parlements might have been getting better at opposition as the eighteenth century continued, but their near destruction under Louis XV oddly caused them to calm down. We've mentioned this briefly already, but the episode deserves a deeper look.

Here's how: the king had been trying to pass greater and greater tax measures to pay off the wars he'd been fighting, and his minister Maupeou and the parlement of Paris (by far the greatest of those bodies, covering a third of France) got into such an argument that the parlement refused to do anything he said, at all. The king responded by exiling the existing members, cancelling all the venal offices which had got them there and filling them with lackeys. He also created more junior courts. When the rest of France's parlements protested they were also erased and rebuilt. The exiled magistrates were not stupid people and they played the public of France better than the king, with the commoners and middle class wanting 'their' parlements back and the power of the monarchy curbed.

Then Louis XV died, and we will never know what would have happened if Maupeou's reforms had continued because among Louis XVI's first decisions was firing Maupeou and bringing the old system back. This probably delayed the revolution. Louis XVI had been persuaded that the public would only accept him if their legal barrier returned, and also it did, venal offices included. But this had two curious consequences: the magistrates of the parlements immediately wielded their newfound essential status and then stopped. They mostly gave up opposing the king and went along with things. But for the public, the illusion of the parlements had been broken. It was clear that not only were they *not* the stout defenders of law that they appeared, because they could be torn down by the king at a brief notice, but they weren't even very good at what they did.

The practice that a centuries' old court would argue with the king, even force him into a few concessions and then claim the moral high ground at a *lit de justice* made the public far more pliant than how they were when they saw a king wiping that court out of the way and dominating. Louis XV was an all-powerful monarch, but he hadn't felt like a despot until he broke parlement. Despot had been defined by Montesquieu as the government of one man constrained by no law beyond his own wishes. Louis XVI might have restored parlement, but he didn't restore the faith in him.

Maupeou had done something else too. With the parlements gone, the people of France looked to other buffers against this despotic monarch, and they found something. The Estates General hadn't met since 1614, and people had only a vague idea of how it worked, but it had once been a representative body with national coverage and details didn't matter: people demanded it come back and solve everything. The calls came to nothing, but a new idea had been birthed, and it would pop up every time the king came into conflict from then on.

The netting which disguised the monarchy's despotic nature had grown huge holes, and everyone in the revolution would look to Maupeou and Louis XV's accidental pulling back of the cover.

A New Mindset: From God to Public Opinion

France was important. I don't just mean in the sense of having a powerful military, because by 1789 Europe looked to Prussia for leadership in that. I don't mean economically, or politically. What I mean is culture, the thing left out of 98% of all wargames. The thing about Europe in the later half of the eighteenth century was that France led the culture of Europe, and all eyes were on France.

Let me explain. With the exception of England, which had spent centuries trying to forget it had been conquered by Normans from France, and Spain, every other major court and aristocracy in Europe spoke French. Even in Russia, French was the language of the elites. If you had money, you wanted French-style paintings and furniture; if you had more money you wanted them actually from France. The ideas, the art, the design of France led the way, and that meant what happened in France would sweep across Europe, and after 1789 it did. What you'll see in this book is that France was such a sun around which Europe orbited that when the revolution happened, firstly everyone would have a view on it, then everyone would act on it, and then the people of Europe would react against French cultural domination. When Napoleon marched, people weren't just repelling *him*—they began to repel a way of thinking.

Thinking isn't an exaggeration. For centuries, the people of Europe had moved along with the same sort of mindset, one which accepted a god and (usually) a king as the rightful rulers, as well as the whole system which went with it. But dramatic changes in culture had started to convulse the European world, from the main Renaissance, through the Reformation and into the Enlightenment, and it's this latter movement which so effects the French Revolution. The exact definition and meaning of Enlightenment and Enlightened thought is argued over, but there is no doubt, none at all, that it helped produce the French Revolution. The arguments tend to be over which part it produced, with a strong vein of modern criticism claiming it produced not just the overthrow of the old regime, but led directly to the Terror too. That will be tackled later, but first: what was Enlightened thought?

The writers who set the tone for Enlightenment rejected old dogma. They valued reason, critical analysis, logic and freedom of thought instead of what they thought came before: blind faith and superstition. While logic wasn't an original idea, dating back to at least ancient Greece, they parcelled it up into a new worldview that believed the truth behind humanity, society and even the universe could be discerned through empirical observation and examination. People, and the world, were rational and so could be understood. This science of man could be used to improve mankind, which gave birth to the idea of mankind's history being a story of progress which could be advanced further. Therefore, education and reason should be used to improve human life and to alter the mechanistic universe.

The large variations in Enlightenment thought usually brought the writers into conflict with the old elites, like the Church and state (although, to be fair, some thinkers allied with the elites to produce a hybrid 'Enlightened Despotism'). Some philosophers had notions of government which opposed the kings of Europe, who they deemed either despots for their rule of 'one man able to do anything he wanted', or soon-to-be despots, because even monarchs who followed codified laws could twist into dangerous ways if the civil state did not form to protect the people. Naturally, there were further variations in what 'good government' would actually be, but one early writer, Montesquieu, argued each nation's state should be divided and balanced between three bodies, this being the best way to keep liberty and order together: the executive, judiciary and legislature.

The thinkers had plenty of material in their attacks on the state. The patchwork nature of France's laws, the tradition which kept old practices current, the one-man rule of the king: everywhere a thinker looked there were abuses of the Enlightenment ideals of equality, liberty and justice. Their writing was voluminous, frequently attacking court cases and grisly executions as a means to expounding greater philosophy. The church came in for as much criticism, as it suffered from the same traditionalism and mixed-up structure, but added a claim to moral correctness which the Enlightenment pointed out was hypocritical.

A group of thinkers developed to tackle the economy, argued for free trade and free production and, consequently, the end of all the tariffs and barriers of France. They were called both economists and physiocrats and they wanted to sweep away and rationalise the economic mess of France just as other thinkers wanted to do the same to the laws and the church.

The mental culture of France was changing, and if you didn't subscribe to the new ideas of the Enlightenment you had to defend what you did believe against it. Writing increased, consumption of writing did too, new methods of thinking emerged and the idea of public opinion now became a common currency openly targeted. People would write to convince the public (in practice, the middle and upper classes) and the government hired people to fire back.

How did culture and this new mental state spread? Partly through literature. France had a thriving industry producing a huge range of reading material, which varied from multi-volume works of considerable size and expense, which only the wealthy and dedicated consumed, to the pamphlet. The latter were small and cheap and produced in vast numbers, their titles and writers coming and going at such speed that the government couldn't effectively censor them, so all sorts of criticism and comment passed. The more incendiary content was printed just beyond the borders of France and main journals were read all the way around Europe. Production and consumption of literature rose hugely decade on decade in the second half of the eighteenth century. The French middle class were vast consumers of literature, including pamphlets. Discussion of key Enlightenment concepts rubbed shoulders with pornography so extreme the internet would blush, despite the official rule that all books had to be approved by the government.

The cultural awakening of the middle class wasn't just through the printed word, which back then couldn't offer the comment sections of today. To discuss ideas (and argue) came societies, of a huge range and variation, which offered meeting rooms, lectures, a library service and a sense of bonding together. Societies ranged from the royally recognised Academies, which offered a home to the greatest people of the day, down through a vast middle tier, to reading rooms which would allow poorer people the chance to read for a very modest subscription, assuming they had the education to read in the first place / at all. Like literature, the numbers of intellectual groups rose every decade towards 1789. While the rulers of France were having problems, the culture of 1780 was rich, scientific, progressive and spirited.

It's worth mentioning that the rural mindset was changing too. In fact, given the pressures that came up from the literal grass roots of rural France and onto the elected representatives, it's essential to note it. Peasants had, for centuries, disliked the state taxing them, but by the 1780s this had developed into an opposition for the dues, rights owing and entire privileged system of the landowners above them. The medieval concept of the protective overlord had vanished, and the peasants had seen their own cultural watershed, recorded their list of complaints in 1789. They were ready to take on their own local elites.

Louis XVI Disappoints

Initially, Louis XVI looked to be a fresh start, a shift away from the debauchery and despotism of Louis XV, but several things soon counted against him. Firstly, he was a king and expected to produce heirs, but a disinclination to sex meant his first, a daughter, was only born in 1778 after eight years of marriage, followed by a son in 1781. The French were used to kings having not just a wife but a string of mistresses, some of which became dominant figures in the nation. The monogamous, seemingly chaste Louis did not fit in.

Neither did Marie Antoinette. As an Austrian royal she was despised by many, and she she was considered a vapid, promiscuous spendthrift. This reputation seemed to be proved to the public's satisfaction in 1785 with the Affair of the Necklace, which is the sort of famous event we need to cover in depth.

The Affair of the Necklace

The Affair of the Necklace has been quaintly called an 'intrigue' but was in reality a con trick against Marie. A Parisian jeweller had created a diamond necklace worth over a million and a half livres, which they hoped to sell to the monarch. However, both King Louis XV and Louis XVI turned it down, with Marie Antoinette rejecting the necklace as against her style. It was at this point when the rather self-styled Countess de la Motte decided upon a con to persuade someone to buy the necklace but take it for heself.

What the countess and her associates needed was a stooge, and they found one in 1785 in the Cardinal de Rohan. He had been an ambassador as well as a cardinal, but had lost status in Austria when he annoyed Empress Maria Theresa, and in France because Marie Antoinette was the empress's daughter. He was desperate to improve relations with the royal family and that opened him up to fraud. La Motte told Rohan that Marie was impressed with him and wanted Rohan to secretly buy the necklace as her agent. Buy it, get it to her and be welcome again at court. At first Rohan was persuaded by a faked series of letters, and he actually didn't realise what was happening even after a staged meeting with the queen (played by a prostitute in disguise, which was pretty much how Marie's enemies would describe her anyway) and actually arranged to take the necklace and ferry back instalments.

La Motte took the necklace away, took it apart and sold it. Rohan waited for Marie to show him some public favour, and grew increasingly concerned when none came. No money did either, and when Rohan failed to pay the first instalment, the jewellers asked the queen directly for the money. Marie knew nothing about this but was now alerted. However, critics have said Louis and Marie should have settled this event in private. Instead, Louis had Rohan arrested, locked in the Bastille and tried in a public court. Rohan was exiled as a result, and La Motte was branded and given a life sentence before she escaped to London. But, and it's a big 'but', while Marie Antoinette was innocent in the Affair of the Necklace and had been shown to be in court, this didn't actually matter. Public opinion took the visible events and turned them into proof Marie was a shopaholic parasite who had just had a cardinal arrested and punished for her own greed. This all fed the weakening view of the crown and increased demands for reform. No one knows what happened to the jewels.

America: France Sees a Precedent

A lot of Enlightened ideas were theory and a lot of these friction points were locked into tradition. There were strong forces stopping change. But then something happened, an example, a precedent: the British colonists in America threw off their far-off superiors and built themselves a new world, with a fresh constitution and system. Suddenly, for every reformer in France, there was a shining example of how the new age of thinking could succeed by removing an old system and produce what they wanted. The fact that the French monarchy had aided the Americans in this was overlooked by both the traditionalists (who were happy they had beaten England) and the reformers (who would take whatever chance they could get). But a number of disaffected French aristocrats had been in America and had seen liberty at first hand. Some of them, chiefly a man called Lafayette, would play a major role in what happened next.

There was also something darkly problematic to observers about France trying to levy new taxes to pay for a war on the side of people who'd been trying to avoid paying more taxes. Why, the thought went, couldn't we be in the second half of that equation?

Many Points of Friction: A Tectonic Fault Line
By the late 1770s France was wracked by forces demanding change. A new generation of literate bourgeoisie were steeped in Enlightened ideas and expanding in number. They wanted rational systems of government, law and economics, but saw only the hodge podge around them that was France. They saw

a king whose ancestor had shown a total disregard for even the pretence of representation. The friction was growing ever more.

A logical search through this chaos to find a solution was in full flow, and one solution seemed to be finding bodies who could act as a check on royal power. Obviously, at this point a national body seemed out of reach, but more and more of the middle class were awakened to new ideas and looking to local, provincial bodies in which they could act. Existing parlements and assemblies were dusted off and invigorated by new blood, and whole new ones formed. France had a late eighteenth-century culture, but the king only had a seventeenth century system to deal with war. Some explosion was inevitable. It's true that the bourgeoisie were growing under the old system, that feudal lords were turning into landlords, that France was slowly changing. But the Enlightenment had given French men and women something to hunger for, and mismanagement would unleash it. The French Revolution wasn't necessary for a modern world, we would have got here, but the French Revolution was how we did.

We'll soon meet a man called Necker, who in 1778 started to create a tier of representative 'provincial administrations' comprised of a quarter each nobles and churchmen and half the 'third estate' (i.e. everyone else). Necker didn't last much longer, but these bodies carried on until the revolution and were closely examined for precedent. The revolution of 1789 came after earlier tremors.

What There Wasn't: Revolutionaries

In 1917, the year of the Russian Revolution, there were men and women who identified as revolutionaries, who had lived for years dedicated solely to the overthrow of the Russian state. France in 1789 had no one like this. There was no concept of the modern revolutionary, and no one of any note was demanding the overthrow of the royal regime. Change, development, reform: all yes. But there was not the type of hellbent revolutionary we now link to the term. 1787 turned into 1789 turned into 1793 quickly but without any planning.

CRIB

- The kingdom of France had been acquired piecemeal over centuries and had massive variations which caused friction points.
- France had overlapping and competing regional governments and law codes.
- Tax wasn't excessive but people in different regions and social classes paid different amounts to each other / one another.

- French agriculture was inefficient and vulnerable to bad harvests, causing considerable hunger, while many landholdings owed feudal dues and services to noble lords.

- A new middle class was growing greatly in numbers and awareness, but they were growing faster than the opportunities in France and were about to wake to the power they had.

- Many opportunities for advancement were in reality buying 'venal offices'. Indeed, almost all official positions in France were purchasable and inheritable, but venal offices were rising in cost as demand soared. Some venal offices made you noble.

- France had a long-established nobility, but they ranged in power and wealth from the well off to a mass no better off than the middle class. Also, a large number of this nobility were progressive and prepared to reform themselves and France, and there were many chances to buy into it. In addition, older nobility tried to limit the influx of new nobility, creating more tension.

- France was officially Catholic, and other religions were viewed with hostility.

- The parlements of France had long been considered defenders of the people against despotic kings, but events around the inheritance of Louis XVI had shattered belief in them. Instead, people looked to a very old gathering called an Estates General.

- The thinkers of the Enlightenment combined with growing literacy and a huge world of print to create a new mindset based on logic, science, freedom and natural laws. The mental culture of France was changing, and it challenged the old regime.

- Louis was disappointing the people by refusing to be a glorious leader, and errors, like the Affair of the Necklace, were undermining the reputation of the aristocracy.

- France helped the American colonists set up a new country, and many saw this as an example of what was possible. Change could happen.

3: The Earthquake: The Old Turns into the New

Turgot Gets It Wrong

It's only fair to pinpoint where Turgot erred as well as had great foresight. The French government had never accepted price fixing as a long-term policy and its agents kept axing it, then bringing it back in a crisis. The harvest of 1774 was so poor that many people might have got their price fixing ready for the inevitable shortage, but Turgot was a man of bold new economic ideals and he allowed a free market which, as you can probably guess, led to rapidly rising prices and rapidly emptying stomachs. In the run up to Louis XVI's coronation, riots began around Paris and a military crackdown was needed to bring peace to the 'Flour War'. This wasn't just the poor rioting but everyone who found their wages could not feed them anymore—the majority of people. Food took up a huge proportion of wages, and small fluctuations left large numbers hungry. The heads of Paris now insisted price controls be implemented, and for several years Paris remained fed, albeit when other parts of France starved and rioted. We shall return to the situation of price controls in Paris soon.

Turgot was right, at least when it came to the cost of fighting the American War of Independence and how that burden would destroy France's chance to reform finances without disaster arriving first... But Turgot wasn't in power for much of that war. An unpopular man, Turgot was edged out and in 1776 Necker became Director of the Treasury.

Turgot is frequently just a footnote, but it's worth mentioning that he wanted to reform the French state, not just the finances. He saw all the fault lines, and wanted to fix them: ending guilds, improving free trade, instituting a land tax for all and more. He proposed nothing less than a peaceful revolution and was thrown out of power before he could really try.

Necker: PR Visionary

Necker had been aiming for this position for many years, and he had been building his image and reputation so well that people were expecting great things. By 'things' I mean not having to pay any more tax. A key part of Necker's plan was a set of semantic and written tricks rather than financial ones. So: he divided the expenses of the monarchy into two categories, ordinary and extraordinary. To his mind, ordinary expenditures (e.g. cost of living) could be met by reforming the current financial system, which is to say leaving taxes as they were while making sure what was coming in was both collected and better spent. Financiers making great profits off this ordinary system would find their profits reduced. Once that was done and France was on an even keel, the king could meet extraordinary expenditures by borrowing.

Most people reading this book have lived through a financial crisis brought on by overextended debts, and don't need to be reminded how debt can be a toxic drain on an otherwise working system, so imagine what was happening in France when Necker declared that France's involvement in the American War of Independence was an extraordinary expenditure. He didn't raise taxes to pay for it, he funded it almost wholly through loans. But loans have interest and have to be paid back, and this interest was shunted over into ordinary expenses.

So, what does this actually mean? Necker was appointed, came with a fantastic PR image and instilled such confidence in the financial system he would run that he was able to secure 520 million livres in loans in just four years. Financial systems live on confidence as much as they live on facts, and Necker was wildly successful in what he aimed to do. Of course, having attacked financiers and become the shining star in the king's ministry, he was in turn attacked by the former and other ministers. So, in February 1781, Necker published one of the most double-edged pieces of public relations of all time, the *Compte rendu au roi*, which was the first time the accounts of the king had been made public. This balance sheet was designed to show Necker and the king in the best possible light, and it claimed that after three years of American war, ordinary income was ten million livres a year higher than expenditure. If you're thinking *What did it say about extraordinary expenditure, like the hundreds of millions in loans?* you're doing better than the many, many people who believed the Compte. It omitted that crucial information. The idea of a public opinion was still in infancy, spurred on as literacy increased and modes of thought changed, but Necker was courting it.

The Compte was successful and destructive at the same time. For Necker, it boosted his popularity and made him feel so godlike he demanded to be allowed into the inner circle from which he was barred due to his Protestant religion. A king listening to Vergennes refused, so Necker quit. The people were outraged.

Necker was followed in office by Joly de Fleury, a man who discovered that so many people believed in Necker and the Compte that the health of the royal finances had been damaged simply by the confidence blow of Necker's resignation. The confidence in royal finances was fading, while everything Fleury tried to do to deal with this vast debt was met by complaints from people who thought Necker had sorted everything and his successors were failures. The Compte created an illusion, a confidence in a system that blocked attempts to reform it.

Fleury raised taxes to do deal with spiralling costs, and people hated him for it. He then borrowed another 252 million livres to cope with the war, and people hated him for that too. By the end of the war, France had spent over a billion livres. A man named Calonne became Comptroller-General in 1783, and the court loved him because he believed confidence in the state could be boosted by spending large sums on showing off, so he didn't hold back the king's expenses and kept on borrowing. This scheme / idea was also successful at what it was trying to accomplish, and hundreds of millions more were borrowed. It's important to explain that France didn't have a single treasury, or a state bank, or a centralised finance point. The loans, debts, holdings, all of it was spread across dozens of independent, profiteering financiers.

It's unusual to say something is successful when we can all see it leading to an explosion, but in the terms of what they were trying to achieve these men *had* been successful: a war was financed and won.

It was only in 1785 that counter arguments began to dig in. In late 1785, the parlement of Paris considered not approving new loans, partly because Necker had published an attempt to justify himself and attack Calonne. It was called Administration des Finances, and it hit Calonne hard, knocking confidence in the system and starting calls for Necker to return. As the parlement had to be shouted at by the king to pass the loan, and as take-up of the loan was slow, rumours swirled that Calonne was about to be fired.

Calonne's Attempted Revolution

He wasn't. In fact, he was about to propose a change of tack so massive it would have been the greatest financial reform in the whole of French history. A change two years in the thinking (it had apparently taken that long for Calonne to get through the voluminous and incomplete records to discover that there was a yearly deficit, it was an entire quarter of the yearly income, and vast debt repayments were still to come). He wasn't a fool, and he knew where the constant recourse to debt was leading. The money available to the crown was going to be worse than decimated as old tax systems expired, short-term war loans came to a climax, and the finances of France found themselves spending almost half their total every year on just dealing with debts.

But Calonne had a plan, a bold, brave plan. He would abolish exemptions, privileges and a whole raft of France's many quirks and replace them with a single direct tax levied on all landholders with no exceptions. This would be assessed and collected by local assemblies comprised of taxpayers, who worked with the intendants (who would remain key). Furthermore, all internal customs charges and barriers would be swept away and grain controls would end. The latter is just three words, but caused an awful lot of concern among people at risk of bad harvests and price rises, i.e. most people. But over time, this plan would hugely increase income, reduce costs and involve the people.

Of course, new loans would be needed until then, which meant Calonne needed confidence among money lenders during a crisis fuelled by money lenders having no confidence. To create the illusion of trust, his plan had a grand concept. He would flirt with modern ideas like representation, not truly understanding the risks, and to create the appearance of national acceptance and undercut any argumentative parliaments, an Assembly of Notables would be called. Calonne rejected the Estates General as too uncertain, and preferred a group of personally invited grandees. These great men would approve all these changes, France would fall in behind, confidence would be restored and reform would progress. The French state would be saved. Calonne didn't expect his Notables to put up any opposition. It's almost like Calonne had never spoken to a group of human beings in his life.

The only reason this doesn't feel like the most earth-shattering, revolutionary reformatting of France's entire structure is because we know what's going to happen next. But the question of how France goes from Calonne's reforms and representation to the far greater developments of the revolution, which unleashed a whirlwind of violence, is one of complete mishandling by Calonne, Louis and others in the upper reaches of the state. Calonne's plan was bold, and it took him a while to persuade King Louis it had to be tried (or else the crown's finances would suck them all into oblivion). Louis finally agreed on December 29th, 1786: an Assembly of Notables was to be called. The handpicked group of 144 people included seven princes, fourteen bishops, twelve people who worked with the Council of State, a few dozen high ranking nobles, magistrates, mayors ... you get the idea.

The French Revolution didn't really start in 1789, although that's the date for essays. It started when Louis declared to his council of ministers that the Assembly was to be called in 1786. Louis had consulted with just three ministers over the calling of the Notables, and he presented its appearance as a fait accompli to the council who would normally have all had the chance to offer input. The king didn't have to call it, but he bowed to Calonne. He also didn't have to call it with such limited support, in a way that alienated many court factions instantly, but he did. Everything spirals out of control from now.

The First Revolutionaries

A notice to the French people on January 29th called the Assembly of Notables, and it met on February 22nd. Between these dates Vergennes died. He had been the dominant minister and influence on the king since the American war was won, and he both backed Calonne and could persuade Louis. His death at this moment robbed the king of a backbone, and Calonne of a man who had kept the financier in power. It changed history.

The Assembly was high born. There weren't even a dozen non-nobles. There were princes, dukes, governors, magistrates, high ranking religious figures. There was also Lafayette, the popular hero of the recent war. Calonne and Louis let them meet in Paris, speak to each other and then they opened the Assembly.

It went horribly wrong for the crown. Louis and Calonne were expecting a grateful group of celebrities to rubber-stamp their reforms, which they only now revealed. Instead, they got a group of people whose complex mixture of responsibilities and emotions meant they could not say yes.

An aside: the offer to the Assembly of Notables was created by Calonne and a team. On it was a man called Talleyrand, who was at this point a member of the church. His skill lay in numbers, not morals. He would appear at key points in French history over the next few decades, as a leading member of the early revolutionaries, as a diplomat, an exile in fear of his life, a valuable official under Napoleon and then an enemy plotting against him, and still into the removal of another king. Talleyrand is one of the era's most fascinating figures, and his involvement started before the Estates General had been elected.

In large part, the Notables didn't like Calonne and would have rejected anything he'd asked of them, to make him beg if needed. The rumours which had swirled round France of Calonne's forthcoming axe were born of a desire to get rid of him. Things didn't start well when Calonne said the finances were in trouble, but Notables looked to the Compte and Necker's recent writing and blamed Calonne instead. However, there was more than personal resentment and the glossier PR of Necker.

These Notables were almost all noble, and they looked at the proposed provincial assemblies and saw bodies they urgently wanted more of their own people on, looked at new types of taxes being levied on the land they largely held and wondered about that. But there was something else, something the crown did not anticipate: the Notables wondered if they had the power to approve of such changes. The new ways of thinking, all those new ideas of representation were surging around France and every Notable could read. Who did they, as handpicked members of France's elite, actually represent? Who could they speak for? And who, once they had gone, would make sure these reforms worked and the finances did not decay again? What would happen to actually change this and who would be the watchmen?

At first they demanded of Calonne the details: they argued they could not accept all these reforms without seeing what this financial crisis was, and on March 2nd Calonne published the facts, showing the much loved Compte to have been a fraud. Shockwaves echoed out, and the next day an idea was vocalised: *we, the Assembly of Notables, do not have the right or the power to approve such revolutionary plans. There is only one body in the French mindset which might, and so the king should call an Estates General.* The members of the Assembly of Notables were the first revolutionaries of this period.

Calonne knew he was losing; the Notables were rejecting him. So he went public. Until now it had all been done in secret, but Calonne joined the call to satisfy the considerable public interest in what this Assembly was doing. At the end of March he published his plans, assuming the people would put pressure on the Notables. The people, however, as well as most of the government, turned against Calonne, and on April 8th Louis sacked him. Louis didn't want the reforms to go, he just wanted someone who could put them through.

But who? Calonne had to be replaced. The first man lasted three weeks and was entirely out of his depth. The next was Brienne, the new Chief of the Royal Council of Finances, and a member of the Notables. Confidence rose, markets steadied; of course a Notable would be able to win over the Notables, and no one was more sure of this than Brienne himself. He worked out a series of modifications to Calonne's proposals which he believed would be accepted and on May 9th proposed them to the Assembly.

If Brienne had done this the day after Calonne was fired, history might be different. But Louis had caused a month's delay and the Notables had been thinking and studying. They had come to want accurate details, not Calonne's spin, and asked for auditors to examine the royal finances. Brienne agreed.

Louis refused. There was no way he would allow his accounts to be examined and he took it as an insult. The Notables took that as a sign they had no power, no actual way of making an informed decision on behalf of France, and shut up shop. They would not rubber-stamp anything, they would instead call for the best representative body they could think of, an Estates General, to decide on the reform of France. Brienne, backed by Louis, closed the Assembly and sent the Notables home, announcing that they would reform France in the manner they wished.

Louis Inflames the Crisis

France was in crisis, no matter what the crown thought. The state had been seen to falter, calling a body of Frenchmen for help then rejecting it, everywhere producing a call for an Estates General to fix what everyone now knew was a sick country. Far from restoring confidence in the state, the affair of Calonne,

Brienne and the Notables showed the world, let alone France, that the king and the leading lights of his realm were in dispute. Brienne carried on. He would pass the reforms, and to do this the parlements had to register them—just the situation Calonne had tried to neutralise with the Assembly. The government he oversaw wasn't entirely spiralling, for legal reforms axed the last uses of torture, but that wasn't anywhere near a leading issue.

The Parlement of Paris was the greatest challenge, and it included no less than twenty-one already annoyed former Notables. Reforms were sent to the parlement, such as the tax changes, and they were rejected and sent back with a call for full financial transparency from the crown and an Estates General to deal with it. Again and again the parlement said *no, give us an Estates General*. But it wasn't just parlement. Ever since Calonne had taken it public, the people of France had been discussing, arguing, debating in pamphlets and meeting places. The conversation of every urban space in France and many rural ones became that of finance, politics and the question of the Estates General.

Then Louis called a *lit de justice*, the ancient procedure by which a king could appear in a parlement and force a law through. Let's be clear here: Louis was proposing something seemingly despotic to enact the most sweeping and modern reforms in French history. It was called on August 6th. Louis slept through part of it, but the people of Paris gathered in a vast crowd to support the parlement's response. They wanted the king given a bloody nose over ignoring them. The members duly did so, condemning Louis and demanding Calonne be prosecuted for financial mismanagement.

On August 15th, the parlement of Paris was exiled by the king to Troyes. Throughout the decades, the exiling of an argumentative parlement by the king had become normal, and the members, at this point, went. This was not a revolution. Even when Paris seemed about to riot, the royal military forced it back down.

The crown hadn't won the initiative back. As the situation in the neighbouring Dutch Republic turned into a Prussian occupation the French crown had to confess the financial situation was so bad it couldn't militarily help its allies in a country which was literally on their border. France had been the dominant power in Europe, and now had to sit and do nothing because the crown couldn't get at the money inside its country. The king, the military, the country: all were embarrassed on the international stage and Britain could smile. The situation in Holland could, maybe should, have been a warning: an attempted revolution saw citizens, oaths, clubs, militias, bloodthirsty press and a lot of things you'll see in the French version. Of course, Holland was near France and the same Enlightenment culture ran through it, albeit with local variations. But although the French Revolution was ground-breaking, it was forewarned by previous events.

Brienne now tried a solution. He came up with a compromise which did some curious things. He scrapped a lot of Calonne's plans and offered to simply have old taxes (and their exemptions) extended instead, and the parlement agreed and was allowed back. This caused an uproar of course, but ultimately this was old taxes continued and not new ones, and the parlement was satisfied. But Calonne promised something else. His whole new proposal was a five-year programme and he said that at the end of it, in 1792, an Estates General would be called to work on the next step. He assumed his five-year plan would have solidified and boosted the French crown so much that in 1792 the Estates General would do what he told it. But first, Brienne had another idea. A show of public backing for the plan. A Royal Session in the style of a *lit de justice*, but without the hard hand of those; a chance for notables to get up and speak at the end of which approval would be given by them. The more things change, the more they stay the same.

Brienne thus walked off a cliff, seemingly completely unaware of history and human nature. The session began, some concessions were thrown like confetti, a demand for new loans was eased in, and people increasingly called for an Estates General to be held immediately. Nearly nine hours of debate passed before approval might actually have been given but then the king rose, ignored everything, said the Estates would meet in 1792 and ordered the loans.

History isn't just huge currents of climate or economy. History is moments of human personality. As the king ordered his loans, rather than wait for them to be given by the parlement, a relative of his spoke. The Duke d'Orléans stated this wasn't legal. Louis, stunned, fell back on centuries of tradition and replied, "I don't care. It's up to you. Yes, it's legal because I wish it." The king stormed off, but the members of the session remained and debated. France was paranoid about despotic monarchs, and here there seemed to be a prime example. With the king now absent, the members of the session rejected proceedings. The king responded by exiling the Duke and others and rejected the rejection of his proceedings. The upper level of French society was breaking apart from the vast stresses. It had come so close to maybe just being okay, and Louis' personal inability to read the world had proved a menace to himself and others.

The king tried to press on with changes, and the parlements and courts of France carried on rejecting them. Reforms, laws, decisions, order: all were bounced back and forth between a monarch trying to force them through and France's great muddle of bodies throwing them back and demanding an Estates General to take decisions. Rumours began that Louis would erase the parlements to a far greater extent than we saw earlier, and the parlements responded by listing true laws and representative needs.

After particularly problematic members of Parlement were arrested, a *lit de justice* on May 8th attempted to crush the parlements and keep France, if not 'absolute' then pretty much the toy of one man. The parlements would be permanently neutered, their powers gone and their memberships controlled. Lower bodies would be given more powers to act as a divide-and-rule counter weight. In addition, the crown published legal reforms so as to appear to be following the trends of history, and a new *Compte rendu* was published to show Brienne's plans were working.

It didn't work. Of course it didn't. Parlements who were meant to change refused, grouped together and began their campaign of opposition. Everyone in the country who could engage in the argument over its future did, and the administrative, political and legal interaction of royal France with the rest of the people stopped. Fights broke out, unofficial resolutions were passed, commanders refused to attack with soldiers. If France in this era had had petrol, May 8th threw a barrel onto a fire.

The crown didn't give in. The army was on side, so the king could do what he wanted as he had the force—but armies need money and France ran out. The royal coffers were growing empty, the debts too big, the confidence in the market too low, the ability to raise loans and pay interest gone. Brienne simply ran out of money and his way of restoring confidence and cashflow was to give the people what they thought they wanted. On July 5th, with France in utter turmoil, Brienne decided to try and call an Estates General on his terms. He set the meeting date for May 1st, 1789 and called for input on what an Estates General would look like, hoping to divide everyone in arguments over this and not everything else.

People cheered, but they did not advance their cash, and on August 16th the royal treasury ceased trading. The French government went into bankruptcy. Brienne, poor Brienne, was aware enough to know only one thing would bring back a sliver of confidence, and he persuaded the king to restore Necker. The hero of the people was reappointed on August 24th; Brienne then quit. But Necker had only come back to manage things until the Estates General.

The Calonne reforms had failed. The Brienne reforms had failed. The collapsing finances of France had seen ambitious men try to rubber-stamp their deeds with appeals to the newly risen god of representation, and in failing to do so they unleashed the spirit of the Estates General. In a sense, the old regime of France had fallen already. The king had run out of money and called a representative body. Louis XIV would have been aghast. There had been no revolution in the sense of what followed, but a history of proud (if arrogant) French monarchs had fallen into a plea for help. There had been no marches, riots or fighting.

The Fault Line

So what had happened here? A combination of war, borrowing and excessive spending had pushed the crown into a financial crisis for which it needed to raise more tax. That, in turn, caused a clash with the leading men of the nation, who resisted the king's demands. This was nothing new. Monarchs had sought more money from elites who had demanded more power for centuries. Ministers had been either avoiding challenging the old system and instead borrowing to push the reckoning away, or determined to tackle the problem, at which point they lost sight of the fact they didn't have the power to both attempt such reform and keep their job in the face of rival noble factions. The makeup of France meant a reform of the tax system wasn't simply about changing the financial structure: the complex interaction of money and privilege, as well as the many friction points and tangled knots of the country's structure meant any fiscal reform needed major political changes too, a vastly larger issue.

But there was a subtle difference with the past, namely that some of these elites were affected by new thinking and refused to do what the king wanted because they did not represent the nation. The king in turn was affected by these new thoughts and tried to break the deadlock—not with a medieval army, but with an appeal to mass representation. In doing this, centuries of power clashes entered a new end game, and the window was opened for a truly remarkable series of events. Louis' tax problems had spread ever wider as people turned outward and invited more people's 'approval' as a solution: from the Assembly of Notables, to the parlements, to the Estates General deputies and electors, then, via the cahiers, to everyone in France, involvement and opinion expanded. Representation had soon been carried everywhere, and with the lists of grievances you'll see in the next chapter, things ceased to be above finance and royal power. It became about the whole of French life.

There is perhaps no clearer sign of how much Louis XVI and his throne wasn't despotic than by this turn of events. Despots aren't supposed to find change impossible, and certainly aren't supposed to become so desperate they turn to an Assembly. The crown of France wasn't a despot, it was a fading power base wrapped up by a tangled ball of steel threads which were refusing to become unpicked. It's also important to remember that the Estates General was supposed to convene, offer advice to the king and then accept the deal they struck and take it back. It wasn't supposed to be a revolutionary body. It wasn't supposed to be a concession bringing collapse. Almost no one thought it would. Advice and approval: that was it.

An Aside: The Day of Tiles

We now turn to the city of Grenoble, home to the Parlement of Dauphiné. On May 20th, 1788 it declared the new laws illegal, backed up by an urban population who both disliked the challenge to the status of their city's parlement, and their own cashflow. In return, the crown ordered the military to exile the members of the parlement, and two regiments were sent under the command of the Duc de Clermont-Tonnerre. Grenoble was not going to take outsiders sending troops lying down, and rebel leaders roused the residents to a fury. A livid and prepared crowd marched to the home of the parlement's president, where the parlement had gathered, to defend him, while others went to the governor's house to abuse him for staying royal.

The Duc, with an alarming lack of wisdom, countered this by sending in small groups of troops who were both armed and told not to use these arms. This went as badly as it normally did throughout human history, as the groups of soldiers were too small to direct the crowds, but large enough to provoke them. Protestors climbed onto buildings, tore the tiles off the rooves and hurled them down at the troops. One regiment withheld fire as ordered, but one shot at the protestors and caused casualties, causing the locals to ring bells and summon everyone to assist. The riot got worse, and the Duc felt faced with a choice of fighting or surrendering, so he reached out to the deputies of the parlement and asked them to calm things down. They, however, felt unable to control the rioters, so the Duc decided to take the route of less bloodshed and pulled back.

The rioters now had free run, so they looted the governor's house, paraded the (actually terrified) parlement through the street and organised a special session. When the adrenaline began to wear off the crowd, some of the older members of the parlement fled the city for somewhere peaceful. However, a body of younger members decided to use the riot for (what they believed was) good. They called for an assembly of all three estates, with the voting rights improved for the third (these concepts will be explained in the next chapter, but basically the magistrates of Grenoble were anticipating the final form of the Estates General). The Duc was replaced, but the next man didn't crush this rebellion either, and events outside Grenoble saw the king have to call a national Estates General.

Grenoble was the first major collapse of royal authority, military failure to coerce, and incident of mob action directing events, and earned the city the claim of being the 'cradle of the revolution'. Royal and military power was beaten by a mob acting in the name of bourgeoisie leaders.

CRIB

- Necker, head of French finance, had borrowed to fund the American War of Independence, but he managed to keep things going because people believed in him. He staged a stunt—releasing the *Compte rendu au roi*—to play on the evolving public opinion and keep the crown borrowing. Necker had, essentially, lied.

- However Necker, a Protestant, tried to move into the inner royal circle, offended his rivals, was fired, and public faith in the system began to decline.

- When Calonne found himself in Necker's position, he realised the entire financial system of the crown was going to collapse, and he proposed a progressive revolution in finance and administration to solve it. He wanted to create a unified system crossing all of France with no exemptions.

- People didn't believe the financial system was failing, because Necker had said it was fine. But spending on war, the money owed on borrowing and French social structures which made raising taxes difficult combined to create a financial crisis.

- Calonne decided to solve this by asking a handpicked Assembly of leading upper-class Frenchmen to approve the plan, which would in turn boost support and allow Calonne to achieve the loans and legal changes needed. Louis XVI agreed and the Assembly met...

- ...and refused to back Calonne. When his own PR stunt convinced them of the need, they demanded reforms and representation.
- Calonne was fired, and Brienne came in to try and revise the plans. He couldn't get an acceptance and the Assembly demanded an Estates General, so the Notables were sent home.
- The French crown was intensely embarrassed when they couldn't intervene in Holland.
- Brienne tried to use the parlements for more PR stunts while altering the royal plans, but Louis improvised and offended everyone, so calls for an Estates General intensified. Brienne worked that into a new plan.
- With public confidence in the crown collapsing, Brienne couldn't get any more loans and the king ran out of money. Brienne quit, and Necker was invited back to run things until the Estates General solved everything.

4: The Estates General

The weather did not cause the French Revolution. But whether you believe in God or chance, the weather certainly did not help Louis. The summer of 1788-89 saw droughts and heavy storms, a winter of biting cold and a spring which did not bring hope. Even if you had no interest in the political goings on, if you cared for neither representation nor reform, you would certainly have noticed the vastly rising grain and food prices from a devastated harvest, the collapse in demand for industrial products as the economy seized up, hunger, unemployment and a France filled with angry people. This had happened before, of course, and Louis' reign was marked by great peaks and troughs of output, but this time it happened as the political classes of the nation seemed poised for a great battle and it fed entirely into it.

A Question of Structure

Necker's return brought peace in name only. The crowds of Paris and other cities were restless, so Necker recalled the parlements, all comprised of men who believed as Necker did that something had to be done to stop the streets from getting out of control. Necker had the insight to realise the reforms would have to be paused, if not cancelled, to give the pressure a release, but he also thought the Estates General would magically make all this okay.

So, Necker brought the Estates General forward to January 1789 and the parlements passed the law swiftly. You might be thinking *Well of course they did, they'd called for that*, but there is a twist. Necker's edict called for the Estates General, but not what form it would take. Calonne had invited discussions on this form to divide people, and he could do so because the Estates was an old institution, uncalled for many lifetimes, from an era where surviving records were not forensic. No one knew for certain what form an Estates took, as it had varied, and the parlements wondered if Necker planned to summon one in a way that made it servile to the king. To this end, they tried to defend themselves by adding to the law that the Estates General had to take the form of 1614.

But there was a problem. In 1614 the Estates had been formed of three groups: the Clergy, the Nobility and the Third Estate (basically everyone not noble or church), each a third in size, each given a third of the votes. That was fine in 1614, but no one of any vocal power had realised this in 1788, and only now did the problem become obvious: the elites—the nobles and clergy—could act together and dominate every vote with a two-third majority. The Third Estate, that is to say the ordinary people, from peasants to lawyers, couldn't do anything without their so-called superiors. The Estates General was massively flawed.

Here's another twist: in the decade before 1788 various local assemblies had formed, mimicking the Estates General but on a very vernacular level. Earlier we looked at the Day of Tiles, and this produced a provincial assembly where Third Estate numbers had been doubled, and all members had a vote each, so the Third Estate could block any votes. This seemed a fairer system, and thanks to the 'Day' the presence of this was widely known. It became an example of what the newly conscious Third Estate should aim for. Of course, this is fractured France, so there was variation. In fact, when the Estates began, and with Parisian deputies not yet elected, it was the men of Dauphine and Brittany who led the discussions—the former wanting to unite with the other two estates, and the latter striking out on their own.

The pamphlets (unique pamphlet production went from the high hundreds in 1788 to the several thousands in 1789), the meetings, the discussion, all exploded in debate: how should the Estates meet? It was just as Brienne had wanted, but too late for him. Necker ended censorship and played along. He called the Assembly of Notables back to 'advise' the king on issues relating to the form of the Estates, and hadn't the parlement of Paris just called for 1614 and a third/third/third split?

The 'people'—the class of literate, debating French men and women deeply involved in new ways of thinking and discussing—fired back at Necker and called for improved Third Estate voting rights. But they didn't just fire back at Necker. Suddenly the parlements had become associated with supporting the old regime with their 1614 call. Suddenly the people of France experienced friction not just with the king, but with the parlements too. The Estates General seemed the saviour, the parlements part of the problem. Pubic opinion, rising like a wave, wanted to double the third. They were led by the Society of Thirty, a mostly noble group of publicly conscious radicals (there were more than thirty of them) who believed the Estates General was vital to renewing France, and who from an early stage knew there would need to be more Third Estate members to change anything. They campaigned hard, and as they comprised what were in effect rebel nobles, they made a deep impression.

It's important to stress here that the revolution wasn't just ordinary people versus their elites. It wasn't poor against nobility. What is so fascinating is that France was so fractured that people from all classes could support all the different things, which was why a good deal of the nobles of France also called to double the third and had, in effect, begun the revolution. Politicians, landowners, aristocrats: many of France's elite were learned, open-minded men who objected to the inherent unfairness of the 1614 system and sided with public opinion. Of course, many nobles clung to the past in the face of all this, and princes and others called on the king to resist the masses. But while the 1614 Estates General had the nobility voting as one block, the 1788 reality is they were anything but united.

The Political Consciousness

By November 1788, French society was highly politicised. Huge numbers of clubs and societies had formed to debate things, while assemblies old and new gathered to urge the king to double the third. Some of the men and women engaged in this argued a high-minded interpretation of representation, but it was easier and more effective to couch everything in class war. The rebel nobles were interested in ending privilege, but the writers found it easier to persuade the masses to want to end nobility. France found a cork had been pulled from a bottle. The middle of France had long been ignored by the ruling classes, and now they realised they would be the Third Estate deputies, they could have a voice, they could reach out, argue, agitate and demand a permanent, decisive role in France and they were utterly thrilled. The bourgeoisie hummed with excitement as their mindset expanded and new vistas could be explored.

In this atmosphere the Assembly of Notables met for a second time on November 6th. It was nervous of the atmosphere in

France. Some dreamed of Enlightenment reform, others were afraid of losing control. The fear won, and the Assembly demurred from approving a doubling. When it broke up, the salons of France abused it. The parlement now tried to win back favour with some carefully worded concessions, but fooled no one when it didn't nakedly state a doubling. Oddly, even the king rejected the parlements, proving that if you can't please all the people all the time, you can annoy all of them in one go.

Necker, wishing to stay popular and avoid a revolt from either the nobles or the people, decided on a compromise. Like so many attempts at this, he produced something which solved nothing. The solution was to reject the Assembly and persuade the king to accept a doubling of the Third Estate. A victory! Well, no, because he didn't decide on voting by head, which rather made the whole doubling pointless. In fact, he said only the Estates General could decide that. He'd kicked the problem down the road. The people were pleased with the doubling, the nobles were okay with the chance to keep the block vote and the fact they could be voted in as Third Estate deputies and fudge things.

The formation of the Estates General was ongoing as France's middle class began to exploit their voice. Debate, argument, opinion: thousands of shades all across the nation. Some of these were balanced and fair, but humanity is given to jealousy and anger, and many voices turned on the privileged classes.

Not with the calm dissection of why privilege was unfair and outright wrong in the new way of thinking, but with anger. Nobles who might have supported the former retreated from the latter.

We now come to Sieyès. He's an interesting man, because in January 1789 he published one of the epoch's defining documents, disappeared from the middle of the revolution and then reappeared, alive and well, near the end where he enabled Napoleon. For now we just need to know he released the pamphlet 'What Is The Third Estate?', an attempt to answer the coming-of-age question in the minds of the bourgeoisie. It called for the ignored people of France to be recognised as France itself, and they should live under a common law of which privilege was the enemy. The Third Estate was the national voice, the patriotic voice, and the nobility, all of them, should be cast aside. Sieyès called on the Third Estate deputies to reject even the Estates General and declare themselves a National Assembly to reform France.

The Third Estate hadn't even had a consciousness a few years before, but now one formed and people emerged to lead it. The most powerful writers (but not necessarily the most eloquent), the best speakers, the thinkers who touched the moment: a group of people from within the new class formed, the natural leaders and deputies. They hadn't existed before, and within weeks they were ready. They were predominantly lawyers because they were the people used to public speaking / debate, issues of obtuse jargon and obvious social importance.

How The Revolution Involved Everyone

The elections to the Estates General were not straightforward. France was still riven by local variation, and attempts to divide it into constituencies were subject to these. You could fill a very detailed study with all these, so suffice to say France was divided, but not easily, into several hundred regions, and each would vote. Each would send two clergy, two nobles and, of course, four members of the Third Estate. But the Third Estate did not all walk through polling booths to pick from a small list. If you were male, twenty-five years or older, you could go to a primary assembly, which chose delegates for a higher assembly, which selected the deputies. If you were poor, tied closely to your work, or had no name, you didn't get very far. If you were wealthy, eloquent and available, you went ahead. You can see why lawyers had a natural lead.

But the assemblies had a second function. They had to write the cahiers. The deputies of France were not expected to arrive in the Estates General unprepared. Cahiers were lists of complaints people wrote to guide and inform everyone of what the people of France wanted. It would be fair to say France, and even the world, had never experienced such a gathering of public opinion, and every single small village was allowed to submit a cahier, which was collated into a master list and sent off. It was a unique exercise, and it made people who were previously uninterested pay close attention. From the royal point of view, it was a mistake of historic proportions. Suddenly people side-lined by centuries of privilege felt involved, were involved. When did the revolution change from something the elites of the country were involved in at a high level, all about finance and politics, to something which involved everyone and everything? The answer is when the cahiers were written, when political change became tied to social issues like hunger, which the masses wanted solved and now thought would be.

Partly by accident, France triggered the most democratic and involving election in European history to that point. Not every election was finished in time for the first meeting, meant to happen at Versailles on April 27th, actually meeting May 5th, but enough were in March and April 1789 to send about eight hundred men out of twelve hundred to the first sessions. They arrived full of hope. This reduced slightly when they discovered the nobles could attend in their most glorious clothes and the Third Estate were given a uniform of black cloth.

Who Were the Estates?

The voting of the clergy and nobility produced unexpected results: there was no top-level domination. The upper echelons of Church 'nobility' found themselves edged out, with far more ordinary parish priests than expected (there were, after all, far more lower ranking religious men who voted for themselves), and their cahiers brought complaints for higher wages and the chance to be promoted, ideas the Third Estate could find cause with. The clergy thus didn't represent the elite estate block everyone imagined (three quarters being lower ranking clergy) but was divided. The nobility found themselves equally surprised when many of the leading men (at least those who stood) found their local power bases selecting 'lesser' but more local men. The Duke d'Orléans made it in, and we'll see him a lot, but many nobles were from the lower ranks and were finding a voice to complain. As with the clergy, the nobility weren't a block of elites but a mixture, including a great many with an eye on reform but worried by the nasty tone of the crowd. As we've seen, most of the Third Estate came from legal backgrounds. Only two could be considered real peasants, and sixty were legally members of the nobility thanks to the quirk that nobles could actually stand as Third Estate.

The three Estates had a lot of demands in common. The cahiers from all estates, and most of the representatives, shared demands for a constitution, the king ruling under law, fairly shared taxation, a regular meeting of a body like the Estates General and other moderate, modern changes. This was what the collapse of the crown's finances and the Estates General had produced. But within that summary is huge variation, some of it within the Estates themselves. Many noble cahiers wanted a retention of the privilege system while bourgeoisie cahiers wanted it reformed, a point of great friction present before the Estates General met, but some nobles wanted the latter too. The clergy were split between those wanting the same type of reform as the Third Estate (such as priests not holding absentee positions). You can pick out a lot from the cahiers and say there was broad agreement, and pick out the rest and say the public opinion of France was dangerously fractured before it even began, sometimes in the same few pages by the same historian.

The cahiers, and the representatives, who met at the start of the Estates General were not explicitly calling for the tearing down of France's entire fabric. They did not demand the erasure of venal offices or even a new and strange religion (which they briefly get in the chapter on the Terror). The demands were great, but this was not automatically the poor versus the rich in a bonfire. And yet, to achieve all these reforms, the tangle of French life would have to be pulled apart, so unconsciously they were moving towards a great reform. The way it actually happened is down to how these representatives reacted to the reactions of the mob. The cahiers were human hope and involvement, and the fear followed to determine the change.

Speaking of bonfires ... we now come to a riot. The harvest of 1788 was a disaster for anyone who needed to eat, caused by awful weather. The agricultural system had already been wracked by a series of bad years, and the response had always been food riots and a demand for grain controls. Over the winter of 1788/9 this happened again, and in Paris people were freezing, starving, angry and spending almost their entire pay packet on food. When a leading industrialist called Réveillon made some unfortunate remarks about lower pay, a riot attacked his factory. What made this different was that the potential representatives of the Estates General took this as a sign that law and order was collapsing in an increasingly violent France. Furthermore, while troops halted the riots, their morale was sinking. This would colour the decisions of the representatives who increasingly felt they had to act to stop an internal war. Reveillon was a sign that the Paris mob was rising and royal power falling.

The Estates Argue

The Estates General opened on May 5th, 1789 in Versailles, palace of the king. Necker gave a speech which history has deemed boring, and walked around the issue of voting rights like a soldier in a minefield. Necker basically told the three estates to go away, ratify their elections, and decide on how voting should be done. If it was to be voting by head, the nobles and clergy had to willingly surrender voting by block. He also decided to add some brazen lies to the situation, as he claimed France was a wealthy nation, the deficit wasn't a serious issue and with just a few reforms it would go away "as if by magic". The supernatural is never something you want your accountant appealing to and the deputies knew he was putting on a show. They knew the situation was far more serious.

The Estates went away and … well, the nobles voted very quickly to verify their order, and they gained a majority of 188 to 46. But the Third Estate had a problem. If you want an idea of how seriously the Third Estate took their chance of rights and power, it comes now: the Third feared that even ratifying their order alone would lead to the three estates voting alone, and so they refused to do even that. The Third Estate agreed to not do any single thing unless all the orders were included and together, and when it became clear the clergy were delaying theirs too (parish priests were proving more progressive than the church elites), they sent a deputation to the first and second estates.

Discussions took place about forming a united ratification, and these weren't quick. The nobility quit them after several weeks. The nobles and clergy talked in secret, but the Third Estate kept their discussions open to the public, providing fodder for writers and visitors. What's vital to remember here is that the Third Estate deputies had not turned up expecting to consign France's structure to a bonfire, as happened later. They arrived wanting certain voting rights, yes, but they were after moderate change and looked to the crown to introduce a programme they could work on. The crown didn't make any attempt to lead (which might have completely changed events), and the Third Estate deputies milled around for a while focusing on voting rights and financial solutions before any notions of National Assemblies and an end to monarchy became ideas, let alone actions. Even as this point, the deputies were not revolutionaries, and were not trying to do that. Events would change things, and them.

King Louis XVI was always going to struggle to deal with these events. His character was not ideally suited. But on June 4th, when the heir to the French throne died, Louis retreated into a morose, doomed state that crippled any chance he had of reacting to this well.

The Creation of the National Assembly

The Third Estates had taken to calling themselves The Commons, and on June 3rd, patience running thin, they elected themselves a Commons president. Many were asking why they didn't just reject the other two Estates and declare themselves the National Assembly. On June 10th, Sieyès, one of the few clergy elected to the Third Estate, stepped forward again to propose just that. A decision was made: a final appeal to the other two Estates, and when that failed, as it did, on June 12th the Commons verified themselves and ignored the others. In effect, the French Revolution had begun as the Third Estate had broken with the law and gone their own way.

The next day, something unusual happened. A number of clergy appeared, breaking away from their estate and signing up for whatever this now was. The cheering was magnificent, and other clergy arrived. This prompted a discussion, yet another one in an endless series but a very important one: this body was no longer the Commons. Now it merged two estates. Could it call itself a National Assembly yet? Sieyès thought so of course, and he guided discussion until the 17th when, with 491 votes to 89, the deputies declared themselves a National Assembly. Imagine the euphoria they had taking this decision—an infant political class finding their voice. And imagine how, in that glorious moment, excited deputies could get the National Assembly to pass a vote saying all old taxes were illegal and would only be kept until new ones were worked out, to keep France running.

That happened, and it marked a direct, unequivocal challenge to royal power: the deputies had gone from being members of a consulting body, to a law-making one. The king set and declared taxes, that was his right, but the National Assembly had taken it from him. Or, at least, tried to.

Louis was in no state to act, devastated by his loss, and the royal response split. The queen supported ministers who started collecting troops around the area. Others supported Necker, who wanted to make concessions and bring the Assembly onside, once again thinking a tame Royal Session could turn them into a usable instrument. Others sided with Louis that the Assembly would break apart and be a quirk soon forgotten.

Necker made a mistake, a strange but crucial one. He arranged for a royal session but didn't properly tell any of the estates. Which was why the doors of their meeting places were locked by soldiers on Saturday June 20th to allow carpenters to refurbish for a session to happen on Monday, and why the estates turned up to find soldiers and chains between them and their new home.

The Assembly had just accepted the formal entry into its numbers of the clergy, and they saw soldiers, so they reacted with fear and pride. They grew angry and decided they must not be stopped from pursing their goal. They found an open space they could use, a tennis court which was soon thronged by spectators, and there they swore an oath, one by one in a grand spectacle, not to quit until France had a constitution and reform. The man who led them to the tennis court (because he knew it was there) was actually Dr Guillotin, and yes, that's the same man who proposed the creation of what became the guillotine. When the Royal Session was delayed to the Tuesday, the Assembly met again to prove to itself it was strong, and they were ecstatic once more as several noble deputies arrived to join them.

Finally, the Royal Session started. The king rose and sleepwalked through reading a thirty-five-point plan which Necker had started but which the divided court had rewritten. If Necker's original government, or Brienne or maybe even Calonne had tried it would have been a document of epochal change and a crown-led revolution. Everything would have been different. No taxes or loans without Estates General permission. But now, after all these weeks of build-up, it was no longer enough. The political climate in France had advanced, the National Assembly had become conscious, and Louis' statement that privilege remained, that feudal dues stayed, that the nobles and clergy could gain a veto, and the closing statement that only he could make laws and reforms valid, not the Assembly, triggered a reaction. The king finished by telling the Session to end, the deputies to leave, and to start again the next day in their Estates.

Many nobles began to do what they were told. Some clergy did too. But the Third Estate and their new noble and religious allies refused to go. One of the newly arisen Third Estate leaders, a giant of a man with a personality to match called Mirabeau, said only bayonets would make them leave, and they began to retake the Tennis Court Oath. Now was the time: would the king order soldiers to eject the Assembly from his hall? His agents rushed to the king to inform him of what was happening.

Louis was not in command, not even of himself. Crushed by the loss of a child, stunned by the actions of his subjects, he had just been told Necker was resigning in the teeth of it all. When asked what to do about the deputies, he did not order force. He said they could stay. Necker was talked into remaining, but not before the news reached Paris, not before the people rioted in favour of Necker and the Assembly.

Many experienced a clarity amidst the chaos: the Assembly was supported by the people. On the 24th, almost every remaining deputy from the clergy joined the Assembly, and on 25th, forty-eighty nobles joined too. Louis didn't just blink, he ducked. On June 27th he ordered all clerical and noble deputies to join the National Assembly. Not all nobles were happy. The heroic bloody mindedness of the Baron de Lupé is a great example, because he simply went to the now empty noble chamber and sat alone in that all day until it was eventually closed, and then sat outside the National Assembly room in a bad mood.

One commentator, Arthur Young, noted that the revolution was complete. This could not have been more wrong. The court continued to gather troops, including units of foreign soldiers believed to be more willing to fight a civil war. The crowds in Paris attacked royal buildings, freeing prisoners and keeping a violent edge burning. The deputies tried to form themselves into their new body, but were afraid and suspicious of the king and the crowd. Necker's enemies at court, who blamed him for all of this, persuaded Louis to sack him, and news of their hero's fall reached Paris just as the devastating weather caused food prices to reach a generational high. Necker was seen as a man who controlled grain prices, who could balance the finances, and he was gone.

This story has, so far, been about politics, nobles and lawyers, hope, ideals and reforms. But now we move to the other great dimension in this tale. On the streets of Paris, the people were hungry and angry, blaming the king for their lack of food, the fall of Necker, the growing presence of troops. They had already been violent, but this violence exploded and people struck royal and religious targets, finding food and then weapons. The people of Paris armed themselves and turned into the mob of Paris, and at the Invalides military hospital they found artillery. The Hôtel de Ville became a base, and one target above all else rose before them. The Bastille. Infamous as a royal prison, it haunted the minds of all rebellious Parisians, who believed it had weapons they could wield, and prisoners they could free.

It didn't matter that the Bastille had only a few prisoners, that it was poorly defended and very underused, that it was a name and not a defence. Gunpowder had been stored in it. Mob representatives first negotiated for it to surrender, but that took too long for the crowd who attacked, and a hundred were killed in a fight. But the mob included rebel soldiers thanks to an ever-growing number of defections, and they stationed their artillery at point blank range. The head of the Bastille knew he had just a couple of days' supplies and considered exploding all the powder (and a considerable part of Paris) before deciding on honour, so ordered a surrender. The crowd surged in, murdered him and took control of a potent royal symbol. A man named Bailly was now elected to a new position: Mayor of Paris, with a new city government and a militia commanded by war hero (and noble) Lafayette.

Back at Versailles, Louis could have been deciding whether to send troops to restore order. But his commanders had given him stark news: the idea of a National Assembly had infected the minds of France's soldiers, and no one knew how many would stay loyal in a battle. If Louis ordered the troops around Paris to restore royal order, he might find himself with no army and a murderous rebel horde. Louis thus took the cautious route, attempted to ride it out, and declared to the Assembly he would disperse his forces.

What did this mean? Royal authority ended and power passed to the National Assembly, but that in turn was protected by the violence of the Parisian mob. The king couldn't control his people, either by words or swords, and he had accepted that instead of a three-chambered Estates General, France now had a single chambered National Assembly who represented a nation, who held power by the will and election of that nation. All attempts by the king and the court to browbeat and harass this Assembly into a different form ended when the mob of Paris pushed the issue and the king found he had no way of stopping them. The French Revolution had begun a few weeks before, but now it had taken a form which would bedevil it for years: a mixture of bourgeois politicians and their uneasy relationship with an armed, violent Parisian mob who had saved the former and would not forget it. Violence underpinned this from almost the very start. Frequently throughout the revolution, the mob murders people. But in a society brutalised by public execution, these corpses are frequently cut apart and carried around the city on the end of pikes. The revolution was dark and brutal from now on.

Aside: The Bastille

Despite being a monolithic structure that was over seventy feet high, with eight towers and five-foot-thick walls, the Bastille was actually smaller than later legend would allow, and hadn't been built as a prison but as a defence against attack. King Charles VI was the first to use it as a set of cells, and the king was able to send people there with no trials, so you ended up with rebel nobles, religious dissidents, writers deemed to have slandered the monarch and people whose families had asked the king to lock them away for their own moral protection. This was how the Bastille developed a reputation as a prison operating outside the Enlightenment ideals of the law. It became infamous, with an image played on by writers and artists, some of whom had been locked inside and reported, or played up, the experience for maximum effect: a symbol of despotism, censorship, torture and abuse.

You might think 'played up' is unfair, as the popular impression of the Bastille was that it was a hellhole. Yet by Louis XVI, the damp, prisoner-destroying cells weren't being used and most people were in the middle of the structure, allowed to bring their own possessions (the Marquis de Sade took a library). You could bring cats and dogs to remove rats, or to talk to. The Bastille authorities were allocated funding for every prisoner depending on their rank, and the three livres a day for the worse off was better than many of the poor outside had. People imprisoned in the Bastille could have an awful time—Linguet's *Memoirs of the Bastille* spoke of being trapped and unable to hear other prisoners—but by the period of this book it was also a handy way to get a career boost. Had you really opposed the king if you hadn't been locked inside? Indeed, the Bastille's time had already come: there are royal court documents from the period before the revolution planning to demolish it and install a memorial to Louis XVI.

When the Bastille fell, the mob found just seven prisoners, including four forgers, two people deemed insane who were sent to an asylum anyway, and an aristocrat.

CRIB

- Once the Estates General had been called, people realised there was a problem: the old Estates had been divided into three 'orders': nobility, clergy and the rest of the people, the Third Estate. But those orders had each sent the same amount, and had voted as three blocks, meaning the nobility and clergy could easily outvote the people.

- A debate began about doubling the third and giving voting by head, and this spread like fire across France as millions came to political consciousness. Plenty of nobility were siding with the rest of the country in calling for this.

- The king avoided deciding on the form of the Estates, and allowed this debate to intensify. What he instead did was invite everyone in France to send in their lists of grievances (cahiers), the largest opinion gathering event ever to that date. This made millions more politically involved, and tied the Estates General to the idea of solving everyone's problems, not just the financial crisis.

- The Estates met. The nobles included plenty of reformers, and the clergy included many lower ranking members ignoring their superiors, while the Third Estate deputies were middle class professionals, such as lawyers.

- Peasants began taking the law into their own hands because they believed the cahiers would be acted on. There was rural violence against privilege.

- The king agreed to double the Third Estate, but left voting to be decided later. The Estates met and were asked to ratify their membership in their three individual blocks. The nobles did so, but the Third Estate feared this would be used to divide them and refused to ratify without all orders together.

- As the other orders refused to come and join the Third, they evolved their thinking and in the heightened atmosphere tensions and ambitions rose: the Third Estate declared itself a National Assembly.

- A confusion over builders led the National Assembly to take the Tennis Court Oath pledging to stay together. Then the king advanced a series of reforms which a year before would have been epochal but by then weren't enough, and Louis was forced to climb down. Clergy and nobles started joining the Assembly.

- The people of Paris, hungry due to bad harvests and afraid the king would arrest the Assembly, turned a protest into an armed riot and ended up storming the Bastille, a royal prison, in search of gunpowder. The king was told his troops weren't loyal enough to crush this and royal power was lost. The National Assembly were now in charge of France and violence was part of the revolution from the start.

5: A Bonfire of Reform

The kings of France had faced a lot of opposition in the past, but never before had they been challenged by a group of people who didn't seek the crown, but instead sought to govern on behalf of the whole people as their elected representatives. To be fair, this hadn't happened much in the whole world either up to this point. The King of France was reduced to travelling into Paris, to the Hotel de Ville, where he gave a number of concessions: troops were being dispersed, Necker would be allowed back into whatever hybrid role this revolution would provide, Bailly (the old National Assembly president) would now be the newly invented Mayor of Paris and the mob of armed protestors on the streets would be given a title, the National Guard, in the hope they could be organised into something less bloodthirsty. Lafayette was appointed their new commander. The National Guard currently numbered 150,000 people, if you gave that name to every armed French man and woman in Paris that day. As Paris and the (revolution-friendly) Duke d'Orleans had long used the colours of red and blue, cockades of these colours were made and Louis put one on. Lafayette would design the National Guard uniform in Parisian red and blue, but with royal white, to make the colours of France ever since, and the cockade became the first worldwide symbol of this revolution.

104

Louis was bemused. Others were horrified. A number of leading royals and court regulars made their feelings known by fleeing France entirely. Throughout this revolution, those who felt threatened would go to the borders, and in time you will see the revolutionaries try and ban people fleeing because the borders weren't just ways to different countries: these countries had armies the 'émigrés' were trying to send back into France.

A lot of elites felt threatened. Those suspected of treachery, hoarding grain (prices were still high), or general anti-revolutionary activities were not protected by the National Guard from being lynched. Across France, violence had begun and continued, as people armed themselves, 'freed' grain, and punished people rebelling against the rebellion. A lot were murdered. In many rural areas the food shortages and food costs meant people took the cahiers as a sign to act, doing so before the king's power had gone. They acted immediately to rectify their complaints, assuming the cahiers would be listened to. The Terror is the most famous act of bloodshed, but death, theft and violence were a part of the revolution from the start.

While urban militias—each town's own National Guard—were pushed forward by the bourgeoisie to organise defence and peace, it soon became apparent to the men in the National Assembly that many peasants had decided 'feudal' dues and privilege should be abolished and were doing this themselves with fire and sword. The countryside was descending into chaos. That was why a group of Breton representatives organised themselves and their club to take control of this violence—to accept that privilege and feudalism were going to be abolished anyway once the Assembly was ready, so why not do it now and bring peace to the countryside? So they organised the Duke d'Aiguillon, a nobleman of liberal views who happened to own one of the largest landholdings in the nation, to make a proposal to the Assembly on August 4th that seigneurial rights should be abolished (in return for compensation) in one massive sweeping vote. The landowners would give this of themselves.

In the period before this, the deputies had discussed whether they had to do what voters had sent them to do (e.g. what was in the cahiers), or whether they could strike out on their own. They voted to set aside mandates, a vote which in effect allowed them to order things people hadn't ordered them to. All of which made what happened next possible, because almost no one had, until then, dreamed of such a thing.

There have been a lot of grand statements in this book, like 'epochal moment' and 'greatest in history', but that's because the French Revolution really was that important and world changing. The night of August 4th is among the most important in history because first one proposal was voiced and passed, then another, and the whole session became a battle of one-upmanship, a bonfire of motions which erased a system that had

106

built up over centuries, which stripped away privilege and exemptions. It was a chaos of self-sacrifice and recrimination. Some accounts will only tell you that men stood and surrendered their own rights and privileges as part of the grand event, and many did, but the opposite was true: people fought. A nobleman would carry a vote ending a religious right so that a priest would have a noble one stripped away and everyone in the chamber went into a state of frenzy to keep scrapping the conflicts of France.

So what had happened? Tithes had been scrapped, feudal dues cancelled but only after compensation had been paid, and when the peasants heard this they refused to pay even that. Peace returned to the countryside because the peasants were very clear that they had won. Venal offices had also been cancelled pending compensation, a simple sentence to write but one which meant every single public office suddenly lost its shape. Promotion had been down to purchasing power rather than ability, and suddenly there was nothing to buy. The chance to have a system based on ability emerged. But this bonfire of dues and the freeing of France did not happen out of grand hope and idealism. Even at this early stage, it was down to fear of rural violence and a desire to save themselves.

Clearly, something needed to be put in place to replace all this. The system might have gone, but the people were still there, and the same. The deputies knew it, and they rebranded themselves the National Constituent Assembly, which would sit until a constitution had been drawn up and a new system of government basically invented and enacted. There was a precedent of course in the new United States of America, and so the deputies worked hard to produce a founding document which would form the basis for everything that went forward. They called it the Declaration of the Rights of Man and the Citizen and they published it on August 26th 1789. It became the cornerstone of French public life.

The Declaration had seventeen sections. They defined the law as coming from the will of the people and sovereignty, nationhood from the same. All citizens were now equal under the law, had rights to employment determined by talent, and tax dues determined by fair distribution. You could neither make laws nor take people away from them (such as imprisoning them without trial) without the national, legal will—not even if you were a king.

The king...

The deputies had reached a fork in the road. They had swept away the old regime and started a new one in its place, but what role did the king have? Did he need to willingly surrender his old powers and declare the new system passed? Would he act as a counter-revolutionary force? Was forcing him to agree contradictory to his new rights? Could it be done without him?

It probably seems strange to read about all the changes and realise many deputies were still tied to keeping a king. Rejecting him was a huge step, and many deputies admired the British system where a parliament ruled in conjunction with a king of limited powers. A faction in the Assembly, who became known as monarchiens, wanted the French king given a veto over the Assembly's decisions, alongside a second chamber of life peers. Understandably, many other deputies thought this was backward-looking nonsense. What then happened was the Assembly rejected a 'House of Lords' but thought their own deep-seated reservations at ending history meant a veto was a good idea, and the decision to give Louis a suspensive one (meaning he could pause laws from happening for several years) passed.

In a sense, the Assembly could not see what a blind alley they were going down, but the people of Paris could and they were shrill in their opposition to the veto. We now come to the first sight of a man called Jean Paul Marat who found his voice, literally, because his newspaper *L'Ami de Peuple* called for the Assembly to be purged of deputies not going far enough into revolution. He didn't just mean making them redundant either. He called for blood.

The October Days

Louis, predictably, didn't want to just pass everything. He saw he had a veto and believed his opinion was being asked, so he gave it. He told the people he would pass some of the changes but not all, he didn't like the Declaration, oh, and he was summoning a loyal regiment of soldiers. The people of Paris went into a fury. The women who had been queuing in markets were able to share their anger, and they marched on the Hotel de Ville, triggering a huge armed march to Versailles, rebel troops bringing their artillery, and when thousands of themm reached the royal capital they stormed into the Assembly hall and demanded stronger action. The deputies didn't have a regiment protecting them and reacted the safest way: by agreeing. The marchers went to tell the king how they felt, and he folded and agreed to pass everything. Only later did Lafayette and the National Guard appear to restore order, and royals openly asked if he had delayed to force the king.

Within hours the king would be a prisoner of the people. A chant went out, then a demand, that Louis should not sit in Versailles, surrounded by soldiers, from where he could react against the revolution. No, the people of Paris wanted Louis in the capital, where they could keep an eye on him and coerce him. Lafayette too asked the king to move, to better protect him and not to have to split his National Guard. The king didn't want to, of course, but when the mob got into a fight with royal guards and were only just stopped from charging into the royal bedrooms, he agreed to the demands. Sixty thousand people processed with the royal family as they marched into Paris and captivity, the result of the Paris mob. The National Assembly didn't take long in deciding to move to Paris too, and they were also now subject to coercion by violence.

Changes

The many different political and administrative regions of France, the bizarre map, was also cancelled, and eighty-three departments replaced them. These were drawn up from scratch to be roughly equal, and had several subdivisions with local elections providing the officials. The king could no longer play favourites, and not even the new Assembly could dominate the activity of the provinces. A mixture of old hands and inexperienced newcomers now ran day to day France. Paris and the great cities had a division called the 'section', with elected leaders. Paris had 48.

To physically defend all this, newly elected officials from the lowest locality to the Assembly in Paris turned away from the army and its royalist officers, and relied upon the newly created, often poorly organised but always overzealous citizens' militias of the National Guard. However, as time passed, these were reformed to try and make them reliable, and so only better off citizens were now allowed to be National Guardsmen, and you had to be able to afford your own uniform, with the hope that

111

sensible, successful people interested in stability would also be reliable.

The old tax system was wiped away and the progressive belief that direct taxation was the only justified system meant a new set of taxes were formed: a tax on land, on 'movables' and on the profits of business. Oddly, such was the hope and zeal of the deputies that they didn't put in place a strong system to collect these... They just assumed citizens would want to pay. They soon learned, as the financial system of France nearly halted, and debts grew as compensation payments kept growing. Necker could not save the perilous financial situation of the state, and the Assembly realised they faced the need to deal with the vast debts which had brought them to this place. Declaring bankruptcy was an option, but that's not a great start to a glorious new era. So as they looked around, they noticed a great source of potential income sat there waiting.

Remember in an earlier chapter when we looked at a huge landowner whose possessions weren't divided by inheritance?

The Church.

The deputies didn't suddenly just take the church lands out of nowhere. There had been a trickle of votes affecting the clergy, such as refusing to name Catholicism a state religion, opening offices up to rival religious factions (such as Protestants), taking away tithes and making priests salaried officials. The church had already begun to be majorly restricted, and the state decided to assume responsibility for relief of the poor, education and other good works once done by religious organisations.

But right from the beginning some voices called on the Assembly to take the lands of the church, and the theory developed that this was justified by the Declaration. It certainly looked like an easy enough solution, and this came to a head when Talleyrand, actually a former bishop, formally proposed all church property be seized, with two thirds given to parish clergy to replace lost tithes and the rest used to pay off state debt. Many argued not to touch the Church, some agreed with Talleyrand, and others wanted to take all of it, lost tithes be damned. In the end, on November 3rd, the Assembly voted to take the land and decide later what to do with it. The debate which followed decided the National Assembly would issue bonds called assignats secured on the church lands, and that 400 million livres' worth of land would be sold with assignats issued in 1000-livre notes which would be used to pay off debts and could be used by the benefactors to buy land. Assignats were not originally paper money, but within weeks they had become it. Assignats in lower denominations were issued and the whole lot made legal tender. However, the temptation to print more and more to solve debt issues meant there were soon 1,200 million livres worth of assignats, far more than the land. Meanwhile, the land sold in 700,000 parcels, and at least one in every eight families in France bought some, although mainly the bourgeoisie. In later chapters you will see how so many of the important families in France wanted an end to the revolution in a manner which left church lands in the hands of those it was sold to, rather than any reversal. There were so many of them, and it was such a big issue, because so many had gained. Necker, seeing a disaster, quit both his job and France.

The Festival of Federation held in July 1790 was to commemorate a year since the revolution. Over forty thousand representatives marched to Paris from across France, where the newly tame Louis XVI (to give a show of old regime subordination), the newly recast Talleyrand (to show support from the church) and Lafayette (representing the loyal part of the military), among others, gave speeches to a crowd of three hundred thousand Parisians. Historian Peter McPhee has called this the "pinnacle" of the revolution. It soon went wrong.

CRIB

- Newly armed Parisians are organised by the Assembly into a National Guard.
- The deputies decide they don't just have to do what the cahiers ask and can go further (the cahiers did not in general call for a revolution!).
- In the countryside, the peasants begin to seize the property of the landowners and destroy the surviving relics of feudal order.

- The deputies, afraid of the rural violence, try to quell it and take part in an extraordinary session in which they wipe away all privilege, venal offices, feudal dues, tithes and the whole friction-causing system of France.

- The Declaration of the Rights of Man and the Citizen is declared and the deputies begin drawing up the constitution of the new regime. Already there is a debate about keeping the king.

- Angered by the king's seeming opposition, a Parisian mob marches to Versailles and, in effect, arrests the king and brings him and his family to Paris.

- The deputies try to solve the financial crisis by seizing the lands of the Church, selling it and using it to create the Assignats which become paper money. Suddenly there is largescale land transfer and a nation of people who will lose greatly if ever they go back to the old regime.

6: Religion Tears France In Two

The Jacobins

Is there a more famous society from the Revolutionary era than the Jacobins? The deputies had split into a mass of societies and talking groups, with one setting themselves up in an old Jacobin convent. In January 1790, they called themselves the Society for the Friends of the Constitution, but they soon became known as the Jacobins. This open, loud, intense society was one of the most famous in the whole of France and local groups from across the nation wrote in to ask for an alliance. By the end of the year the Parisian Jacobins were affiliated with over two hundred local societies. The Paris Jacobins weren't purely deputies, although they quickly counted over two hundred among their number, but a thousand learned citizens of France all engaged in passionate idea sharing and discussion. Debates would be held in the convent before Assembly sessions, with the deputies taking ideas with them, and then again after to expound on what the Assembly had said. The local societies looked to this hub for leadership.

Religion Breaks the Consensus

The reforming of France soon showed how wholesale changes made through the prism of human nature (fear and sacrifice, jealousy and benevolence) could bring problems. When former

116

members of the religious estate got up to speak now, they were jeered, and the motivations behind the dissolution of the monasteries was partly the judgement of people, parish priests among them, who simply hated monks. The latter lost their lands, then lost their right to exist. Many Catholics in France, including those in the Assembly, wondered if this was all going too far, because Catholicism was being neutered and transformed, while Protestants seemed to be gaining ground. The violence which started over the kingdom had religious elements—Catholic groups versus Protestants—and a sectarian tension spread from the reforms.

There comes a time in many histories of Europe when we say, "And now the Pope appeared", and this went as badly as it usually did. Within France was a Papal enclave called Avignon, which had once been the official home of the Papacy and which now did what the Pope told it. When the Assembly began reforming France they didn't just end France's payments to the Papacy, they triggered the patriots of Avignon to demand a return to French rule, and when the Pope condemned what was happening in France, these patriots seized power and declared Avignon for the Assembly. Obviously the Pope wasn't pleased, but he was about to become apoplectic.

The Assembly hadn't just been stripping the Church of rights, they had created a committee to draw up a future format for the Church. They wanted to specify funding, who had what rights, how it worked: a plan for the future of French Catholicism. This plan was drawn up mostly by people from outside the clergy, and operated on the principle that the ultimate authority in the French church was now going to be French, and not, very much not, a Pope. They also had no interest in asking the clergy within France to discuss their decisions in anything other than the National Assembly, even though there was a call for church bodies to examine it.

The result was the Civil Constitution of the Clergy, a mixture of common sense, streamlining, listening to the cahiers and completely ignoring tradition or how this could all go wrong. The map of parishes was redrawn for maximum efficiency (which meant far fewer parishes—Paris lost nineteen of fifty-two) and the pay was, for most, good. But it also, in the traditions of meritocracy and representation, stated the clergy had to be elected. By the parishioners. No permission or escalation to the Pope was possible. While few of the clergy outright opposed this in order to stay onside with the revolution, they did want the Pope to agree to it, whereas the Pope thought it was a terrible idea and decided to refuse to reply in the hope of the constitution failing due to internal opposition.

The Civil Constitution of the Clergy was passed by the Assembly easily enough. Then, thirty deputies who had voted against, all members of the clergy, restated in an appeal to public opinion that either the Pope or a Church Council should agree to this first, and the situation exploded. Tensions had been running high, but those upset at the effects on the Church, and those loyal to the old Church, protested. They found themselves attacked by a group of angry, militant activists led by members of the Jacobins. Many of the priests rebelled and refused to play along with the changes, the elections fell into chaos, people were dismissed and replaced, and the Assembly watched their new law bring disorder.

The Sundering

They deputies reacted with a heavy hand. Rather than be conciliatory and find a way to deal with the old Church, they ordered that every member of the clergy who didn't take an oath accepting the new regime was to be fired and replaced under the rules of the constitution. The king passed the law, afraid to reject it. The result was to split the people of France into two passionate, vastly divided blocks. The attempt to reform the Church had run into predictable opposition, but the oath given to the clergy shattered any pretence of consensus and caused a literal civil war among the French people. No longer was the revolution about the old regime and the new. Now it was a chasm among the people. Why? Because half the clergy refused to take the oath. They became known as refractories. There was vast regional variation, with Paris swearing and the west of France refusing. Talleyrand, a bishop and a born survivor, was one of the few bishops to take the oath and provide a lovely veneer to the chaos. Violence flared, as it did so often with this revolution. When the Pope publicly declared opposition to what had happened in France, Parisians burned models of him. Others took heart in their refusal. Catholicism and the Christian Church in France had separated and become two different things.

Counter Revolution

The Count d'Artois had fled France to set up a counter-revolutionary campaign, a rebellion to the rebellion. He was a fantasist with little power and his plots came to nothing. Louis even told him not to mess about and cause trouble. Indeed, there was no serious counter-revolutionary activity in the early days of the Assembly. Even the skulduggery of Mirabeau—who was considered to be a leading deputy by the patriots, but who was secretly being paid to advise the king and aimed to have him moved out of Paris as a strong figurehead for the redrawn France—had little practical effect. When it was discovered he'd advised the king that civil war might be a good idea, even the fact he'd died by then didn't save him.

In fact, the king was in far more danger than the revolution. Crowds of anti-royalists had to be stopped from threatening, marching and even rioting by the National Guard. Lafayette was in charge of the Guard, and he warmed to the royals, but Louis and his court began to know they were prisoners in Paris and desire an escape, while the mob of Paris began to suspect any royal movement as the start of a flight plot. With the situation collapsing, with the mob stopping even a small planned holiday for the royal family, Louis began to actively plan to flee. At the same time, refractories and their supporters turned back to the king as the ultimate hope for a reversal of the revolution.

France was boiling. The tension wasn't just over religion and royalty. Unemployment was high, and the Assembly had axed the guilds so workers and bosses were engaging in bitter disputes over work and wages. Then the Assembly passed a law banning trade unions.

Why? The law came from a former leading Jacobin, Le Chapelier, and found support from deputies who agreed with him that the revolution, while it had done well, was about to go too far and the status quo had to be rescued. He and these like-minded men created a society in opposition to the Jacobins. They called it the Monarchial Club. You can see who they wanted as the head of their state: the king. The Jacobins were accused of wanting the opposite, namely the king removed from all power and the people as the supreme head of France. Their leader, although probably not a hard-line republican yet, was one of the most infamous and fascinating revolutionary figures. Robespierre. His first legal move was to draft motions which banned the deputies from taking executive power after the

121

Constituent Assembly ended, and similarly prohibited members of the Constituent Assembly from moving into the Legislative Assembly. This was all to do with making sure no one could build themselves a dictatorial power base, which was one of those glorious ironies because it was Robespierre who would do just that first. Robespierre then tried to have France annex Avignon, but failed, campaigned against slavery and won rights for the previously oppressed. He was noticed by the people of Paris.

The Flight to Varennes

We return to Mirabeau. For weeks after they had been side-lined by revolution, the royal family had been paying for his advice. A giant physically, with a voice to match, this once dissolute revolutionary positioned himself as a potential first minister between the king and the Assembly, and saw nothing suspicious about being paid to give advice in secret to the royals while largely running the revolution. He suddenly died, and was hailed as one of the true heroes of a revolution searching for them. Mirabeau's death had two consequences. The first was the king changing tack without his advice, and engaging in the adventure in the next paragraph. But the second was longer term. So much of the next few months and years happened because of human fear and paranoia. When the details of Mirabeau's advice and the king's payments emerged,

Mirabeau's memory was disgraced and so one hero of the revolution was turned into an enemy, feeding this paranoia. Mirabeau's death leftbehind a land mine that gets stepped on in a few chapters.

There is a basic truism that if you're going to write a manifesto damning a revolution and leave it behind when you flee, it's a good idea to succeed because when you're brought back and people find it, you're in a lot of trouble. Which is basically the royal family's flight to Varennes in a nutshell. The king wrote a document criticising everything that had happened, and then an 'admirer' of the queen, Count Axel von Fersen (who was Swedish), arranged things: the royal family would disguise themselves, board a coach, travel north through France to the border, meet up with a loyalist royal escort, then escape the country. On June 20th, at night, the family did just this; sneaked past the guards and rode away.

But the escape had been delayed, and the royal party only reached their first rendezvous when the escort had already left, assuming the plan was off. They rode for the next rendezvous and eventually paused in Sainte-Menehould on the night of June 21st, still without guards, where the postmaster recognised the king, rode to Varennes to sound the alarm, and everyone was arrested. They were escorted back to Paris, by which I mean ordered.

If the oath of the clergy had divided the people of France one way, the king's flight divided them another way. It had been easy enough to move forward in reform by just mentally moving the king to one side and assuming he could be told what laws to agree to. Most people assumed the forthcoming constitution would have the king at the top, just with little power. But now this king had betrayed the revolution, rejected it and tried to escape. He was seemingly opposed, and everyone in France had to decide if they were for the revolution, or for the king. The oath and the flight forced France to split into camps which would fight each other.

Paris rose in republican fury, attacking royal symbols, and thirty thousand Parisians marched to support the Cordeliers Club (who were more extreme than the Jacobins) and their demand to depose the king. Across France the National Guard readied themselves for Austria to attack (because the queen, who needed saving, was Austrian). With no immediate signs of invasion, they harassed refractories and royalists instead.

The National Assembly, however, were afraid. They had almost finished a lovely constitution with a king at the top, and bowing to republicanism would be bowing to the Paris mob. They didn't like that, so in an early example of fake news / outright lying for PR's sake, they pretended in a proclamation that Louis had been abducted, that he hadn't wanted to flee, and, yes, while the king's powers were suspended, he wasn't against the revolution. Bizarrely (or perhaps not), the Assembly managed to get away with this for a while. A short while later they imposed penalties on the 'émigrés', the people who had fled France and the revolution, drawing up lists. The émigrés included, within a few months, half the army's officers. It had ceased to function.

The Jacobins were damaged by this divide. Jacobin numbers had risen, and republican societies in France urged the Paris Jacobins to nakedly call for a republic. When a swiftly written document did so, the Jacobin members split: monarchical minded members quitting to form their own society, the Feuillants (named after another convent). The Jacobin club was sundered, and left behind was a small number of deputies led by Robespierre.

One of the people who'd quit the Jacobins was royalist protector Lafayette. When the Cordelliers held an event on the Champ de Mars on July 17th for thousands of people to sign an anti-royal manifesto, a handful of royalists were lynched and the Mayor of Paris, Bailly, declared martial law to stop it. Lafayette and his National Guard marched to break up the gathering, but a fight began and the Guard retaliated, leading to the deaths of several dozen in what would be known as the Massacre of the Champ de Mars.

Journalists like Marat were already calling for blood. He, in particular, felt that cutting off five or six hundred heads earlier

125

on would have saved needing to murder the numbers he was calling for now.

In the bloody light of the next day, it looked like republicanism was gone, its members fled abroad or hiding, its clubs reduced in size, its people on the street, dead. They couldn't have been more wrong.

Europe and the Declaration of Pillnitz

Europe was watching the revolution. No one had predicted this would happen, and in 1787 and 1788 the rival courts of France and the thinkers in their coffee houses alike all viewed with interest how a weakened France had been forced to step away from international relations because of financial insecurity. But no one expected to find, in 1789, a National Assembly with control of the once great nation.

It was then that the French Revolution became the viral video of its day. The eyes of Europe turned to France and lapped up any and every report of the remarkable events. For nationalists, thinkers and rebels across Europe, France suddenly became proof that change was possible. For monarchs and members of the old regime there was confusion as to what had happened, but a wry smile that France had fallen behind their own (sometimes great) nations. There was surprise, and opportunity: a new French regime might support you, if you courted it, or be too weakened to oppose you. The Dutch in particular, mired in

126

a conflict the French had been forced to stay away from, saw multiple paths forward.

In Belgium, the revolution had its first domino effect. Austrian Emperor Joseph II was involved in a struggle with locals and rebels for control, and when the latter saw what was happening in France, they began an attack which overcame the Austrian forces stationed there and allowed them to declare, on January 10th, 1790, the United States of Belgium. The rebels promptly fell into an argument, with those wishing to reformat the nation in the French manner forced to flee to France. Meanwhile the remainder—conservative but anti-Austrian— braced for Joseph II to arrive… But he died, and Leopold took over. In one sign of how the revolution developed, and how people didn't see where it was going, Leopold initially praised events in France, writing in 1789 that all nations would have to copy the French example, and it would bring happiness.

If you're wondering why you've never heard of the United States of Belgium, that's because it didn't last a year. Leopold's wonderful reforming credentials didn't really survive coming to power, as he first offered to let Belgium stay the USB if they accepted his sovereignty, and when they didn't he made a deal with Prussia, marched in and crushed it. The rebels fled … to France, where the other Belgian rebels weren't entirely pleased to see them. The Belgian rebels had looked to France and the National Assembly for help, but it hadn't come. In fact, the latter had voted never to fight offensive wars. Hold that thought, it changes very soon.

Prussia, Austria and former rival monarchs were wondering how to react to France. But while the deputies might have been afraid Leopold would march into France to free their family (Marie Antoinette), and while many generations of readers have assumed the same thing, Leopold actually looked at France, nodded, and turned his attentions to a prize: Poland. At the time, Prussia, Russia and Austria were circling and they would soon complete carving it up between them, in a conflict where Polish patriots had been stirred by France, but were far from copying the ideals. Poland seemed a far better place at this point to direct Austrian and Prussian troops and money.

Some money was spent on France, but not on a huge army and invasion. It was instead spent on the people pleading for a huge army and invasion. The émigrés who fled France included nobles, military officers and people ready to agitate, and they clustered together in Trier (where Artois' uncle held power) and Mainz. They were paid pocket money by the rest of the European states to maintain their status as troublemakers and no more than a rag-tag of adventurers.

Then Leopold did something, in concert with his fellows, which achieved precisely the opposite of what they were trying to do. He met King Frederik William of Prussia at Pillnitz in Saxony, to discuss how the revolution was threatening their family and thrones. On the one hand the émigrés, as well as a strong body of Western European public opinion, was demanding one or the other (or both) these men intervene to restore the French king at the front of an army. Artois and Calonne had united to try and become opposition leaders and when they heard Austria and Prussia were meeting to talk, they tried to get an invite, got no invite, turned up anyway and got the resulting agreement to refer to them.

On the other hand, Leopold took the view that threatening France would actually increase the danger to his sister and brother-in-law, rather than reduce it, and he wasn't rushing to increase the tension in his own fractious empire with a war in France. Only when he thought Marie Antoinette and family had escaped France beyond Varennes did he offer all his resources, an offer withdrawn when he discovered they were prisoners.

The Aims of the Declaration of Pillnitz

Prussia and Austria were far from allies, but at Pillnitz they reached agreement and put out a declaration. The thing about the Declaration of Pillnitz was that it was a diplomatic document using old regime language and so had a double meaning. At face value it was a rebuke and a threat to the revolutionaries in France, but a close reading of the words meant, in practice, it limited calls for war, slapped down émigrés and supported the royalists in France. So, it stated that the French Royals were of "common interest" to other monarchs, urged France to restore them and made threats if they were harmed. But it also said Europe would only act with force if all major powers agreed, and as everyone was meant to know Britain wouldn't do that, this meant no one was threatening anything. It was tough but empty. The Declaration of Pillnitz was written to aid the royal faction, not to threaten war.

The Reality of the Declaration of Pillnitz

Unfortunately, the revolutionaries were no longer working in the realm of old regime diplomacy. The deputies and the press had developed a culture that erased subtlety and spoke in absolutes. For them, oration was all about moral black and white, passionate statements of pure truth, and any cleverly written subtext was wrong. So the revolutionaries, especially those who wanted rid of the king, were able to ignore the real intent of Pillnitz and use it entirely at face value, as a threat of invasion to scare people with and push them into extremes. Pillnitz was an utter failure.

CRIB

- The deputies introduce changes to the relationship of church and state which creates great opposition.

- The deputies' response to opposition is to demand the clergy take an oath of loyalty. The effect is to shatter the revolutionary consensus (such as it ever was), and to divide France into loyal old school Catholics and new priests.
- Meanwhile, émigrés who had fled France are plotting to find support and troops to march back in.
- Having once more been threatened by a mob, Louis and his family try and escape France in the Flight to Varennes, but are arrested and returned as prisoners to Paris.
- Louis left behind a document attacking the revolution, and the deputies have to lie to keep peace and blame from the king. They all pretend he was kidnapped.
- France again divides, this time over whether they consider the king a friend or an enemy.
- Austria and allies issue the Declaration of Pillnitz, an attempt to bolster the French king's position, but it just ends up annoying and radicalising the people of France.

7: The Fall of the King

The deputies of the Constituent Assembly continued to work on their constitution and continued to keep Louis in it. But he was now to be the newly coined 'King of the French' and he would have no significant power. He couldn't write laws, he could only block laws with a veto for three years; he could appoint ministers but the deputies of the new Legislative Assembly could fire them and they couldn't come from that body. The new Assembly would have 745 deputies sitting for two years, and would be voted for by something called active citizens. These were men over twenty-five years of age who paid the equivalent of three days' unskilled wages in tax. The effect was to limit voters to the bourgeoisie and above, shutting out the mob of Paris and the peasants around it. Only 4.3 million people could vote, and all they voted for was electors, people who paid ten days in taxes (only 45,000 people.) The electors in turn went on to vote for the deputies, who had to be paying 54 days' worth of labour in taxes. It didn't even look good to the masses of France at the time, let alone now. But there was a system to solidify all this; active citizens also voted for all public offices except ministers, e.g. judges and priests. The parlements, and all the old systems of courts and government vanished, to be replaced by a new one which would hopefully one day create a universal law code across all of France.

Then, writing done, work on the constitution was finished. Some concessions had been made to try and make it work: the Civil Constitution of the Clergy was kept separate, so a vote or an oath to the constitution could be made by refractories, hopefully garnering widespread acceptance. Then it was presented to the king.

He didn't immediately accept. He twisted and turned. The Feuillants were active, trying to rebuild support around the king. Louis only accepted the constitution after ten days of thought, on September 3rd, so the Constituent Assembly ended on September 30th. It had done a huge amount, in terms of ending a centuries' old regime and rebuilding France. But it had left the nation broken down the middle by the way it had treated the Church, and the way this had triggered the flight of the king and the damage that did. The Constitution of 1791 was in no way prepared to deal with this friction.

To celebrate, an amnesty was announced to pardon those guilty of crimes against the revolution, which caused a lot of criminals to suddenly become politically more active than they'd previously been. No points to Rabaut Saint-Etienne who wrote: "Most of France is settled … the moment has come to write the history of the revolution."

The Road to War

The Legislative Assembly opened on October 1st 1791. Unlike the three orders of the assembly which had created it, the legislative one was almost entirely bourgeoisie. The priests and nobles simply hadn't stood for election, and the men who had been most vocal in their local areas during the months of the Estates General and Constituent Assembly had instead come to Paris to take over. They were mostly lawyers and other people trained in processes and public speaking who had been the core of local societies. They began by tackling what they thought was the main problems in revolutionary France: refractory priests (for whom they wanted to pass more powers to coerce into submission), and the ever-present Sword of Damocles that was the émigrés. If anything, more people than ever were fleeing France to the rebel enclaves.

One problem that seemed to be settling down was the king. His reaction to Pillnitz was to plea for émigrés to return to their homeland and follow his lead in making the constitution work. This might not have convinced your average Jacobin, but when the new deputies arrived in Paris, far more of them joined the Feuillants than the Jacobins. Indeed, the royal family seemed to be listening to the Feuillants, so although its former deputies couldn't be Legislative Assembly members yet (due to the rule blocking a straight move there from Constituent), they had stayed to act as the king's guide. Unfortunately they made a major error. They met and discussed in private.

Public opinion was a vital aspect of this revolution. The Jacobins met publicly and could build reputations across Paris (and thanks to the network of societies, across France). Anyone wanting to build a name joined the Jacobins and competed with star turns like Robespierre (now an official in the Paris legal system). Indeed, Feuillant membership declined as people turned to the more famous Jacobins. When the Feuillants did finally open their doors to compete, they were found bland, wanting, and unable to defeat hecklers.

It all went wrong for Louis and the Assembly, of course. Jacobin leaders in the latter persuaded it to pass a law ordering all émigrés back, else their property would be seized. But Louis refused to pass the law and used his veto. He allowed the Feuillants to create what was basically a press release explaining why he refused, but the schism of king and government was reopened. Then it got worse. There had been more violence, as there frequently is in this story, and in Avignon pro- and anti-refractory citizens had fought. People had been massacred in a prison (this will soon happen again and again on a larger scale). The Assembly response to the division of France between the old and the new was to stamp hard on the old, so to deal with the Church they proposed a new law and a new oath: anyone refusing to swear was to be a double refractory, deemed a suspect, spied on and, if necessary, exiled. The deputies had responded harshly to doubt and division with fear. At the end of 1791, the king vetoed this too.

Louis had not sat idly by, but he wasn't acting in the way deputies hoped. They had asked him, in his position as head of state, to threaten neighbouring places called Mainz and Trier with French armies if they didn't stop helping the émigrés. Louis was convinced that if the French army attacked anyone in its current state it would be defeated and the Austrians and émigrés would come charging back to Paris—which was the opposite of what the deputies wanted but appealed greatly to him so he made the threat! The Jacobin deputies expected a glorious military parade of national renewal, the monarchists (and the king) a glorious defeat. Then the heads of Mainz and Trier did as told and kicked the émigrés out and almost everyone was disappointed.

Robespierre wasn't. Still vocal, growing in fame, he opposed a war because he feared a takeover by the generals, monarchist or republican (he would be proved right in the end). But he wasn't in the Assembly now. Instead, the Jacobin leaders there, joined by many other shades of deputy, had seized on the idea of a war of national renewal, a march of freedom across Europe and an explosion which would reveal in France who was loyal and who was a traitor. Deputies began to see war as ideal and constructive, a solution to division by wiping away the other side.

Back in Austria, Leopold was getting some bad advice. A combination of errors made him think that he should respond to the ultimatum against Mainz and Trier by threatening an invasion of France if the French attacked. So he did. This was exactly what the pro-war parties in France wanted to hear: a justification for war. They demanded a declaration against nothing less than the Austrian empire. Robespierre's supporters and Feuillants alike shouted 'no'. They weren't heard. Louis was ordered to send a threat to Austria. Still expecting to be saved, he did. But he was operating under old styles and sent a low-key note, then two things happened. Firstly, the arguing factions in France forced Louis to appoint a government of 'hawks' to wage the war. Then Leopold died of unrelated causes.

The hawks did not care. Francis II replaced Leopold. Louis declared war on Francis. It's worthwhile looking at the various aims of France: to stop Austrian involvement in France, to ruin the émigrés, to ruin refractories and French anti-revolutionaries, to unite France together and distract from problems at home (more food shortages, more violence, open conflict between revolutionaries and loyalist rebels). Also, if you were the king, to see French armies beaten and the revolution battered.

The declaration was not caused by grand, impersonal forces like famine or economics; it was a decision made by humans, a result of their personalities.

The War Goes Wrong

The history of war is littered with examples of naïve—stratospherically naïve—politicians ordering wars to unite nations and solve internal issues, and for this to initially work as the nation binds together and armies march off for glory, and for that last until an hour after contact with the enemy, at which point it all falls apart. This was no different. Soldiers cheered, civilians cheered, the old enemy of Austria was the enemy again and France was going to humiliate it. True to historical form, a cheering army marched into Austrian-controlled Belgium, which they thought would welcome them with open arms. But they found opposition, got into a fight, and ran away. But not before killing their own French commander. This was an omen.

Austria, now allied with Prussia, wasn't moving quickly, and this left a period for France, particularly Paris, to stew in paranoia and fear. The thrill of an army leaving turned instantly into the fear of recrimination when the Austrian counterinvasion would hit Paris, and these human weaknesses were turned on those around them. War advocates blamed anyone but themselves: the king, the generals, the monarchists, the refractories, the émigrés. As with any war, foreigners were targeted and all of those in Paris were to be spied on. Refractories were to be deported. Soldiers around Paris, including a force of royal bodyguards, were to be sent to the war zone and replaced by the supposedly patriotic National Guard.

The hawks were arguing and gnashing teeth, so the king asserted himself. He threatened to veto these laws, sacked a number of ministers and replaced them with Feuillants. This caused a deep argument about leadership, with everyone pointing fingers at everyone else: coups, betrayals, threats.

It wasn't just deputies and ministers attacking each other. The people of Paris were watching. They heard about military failure, but saw the king remove ministers. They were afraid of a counter reaction, and the Cordeliers society, still extreme, organised the people into a demonstration intended to get all of the war party back into power. They seized on a planned planting of a Tree of Liberty in some gardens known as the Tuileries to mark the Tennis Court Oath, but everyone knew this wasn't going to be peaceful banner waving.

The mob formed on the morning of June 20th and acted, changing the course of the revolution again. Tens of thousands gathered with arms, arrived at the royal palace, entered it and marched into the king's apartments. He was barely defended but stood his ground as, for two hours, the citizens of Paris streamed past him shouting invective. They called themselves 'sans

139

culottes', in reference to the fact they didn't wear knee-length breeches and stockings like the rich. Louis kept strong, said he was loyal to the constitution, and finally the demonstrators went home and the ministers remained unchanged. Louis had, in the short term, won, but in the long term everyone was preparing for another armed confrontation, one which would not end well.

The Assembly pulled huge numbers of National Guard close to Paris. Part of this was under the cover of anniversary celebrations, and partly under new laws declaring the 'Country in Danger' and demanding a spirited defence, a demand which was optimistic given how poorly the offence was doing. It was at this point that volunteers from Marseille arrived in Paris singing a fight song by Rouget de Lisle which became globally famous and known as La Marseillaise. These patriot civilian soldiers were approached by republican societies, like the Jacobins, and drafted into the struggle. People spoke of removing the king's veto, or even the king himself. But the republican leaders were careful, and wanted the next attempt to succeed. So, the National Guards were damped down whenever they seemed about to act, and the activists used the 'sections' of Paris (the administrative units the capital was divided into) to organise opposition. A web was bound together, and leaders like Robespierre led them.

We now come to the other great failure of Revolutionary era diplomacy. France created four armies to form a defensive barrier, and by the middle of August the main army of the anti-French coalition had entered France. It was led by the Prussian Duke of Brunswick and had 80,000 men. Capturing fortresses such as Verdun, it closed on Paris, making the Army of the Centre look a disaster. This caused terror in Paris...

The Duke of Brunswick tried to threaten the people of Paris into leaving the king alone. He'd heard about the march on the Tuileries and in a proclamation as ill-advised as Pillnitz, ordered Parisians to respect the king and his palace or else he would exact "forever memorable vengeance". Naturally, when the Assembly read this they did the exact opposite, which was to issue Parisians with weapons and allowed, demanded, everyone to join the National Guard. A body once dominated by men with property and alleged caution was now filled with the men of the mob.

What came to be a last attempt at using the Assembly was made. The deputies were urged to prosecute Lafayette with betraying France, and they refused ... but they knew what that meant. The republicans outside the Assembly triggered the mob they had carefully arranged, and on August 10th the tocsin was sounded to start a revolution. The central committee of the Paris sections declared themselves a commune and ordered the National Guard to march on the king. Louis and his family rushed to the Assembly hall to take shelter with the deputies, who looked on in horror at having lost control. A mob arrived, the Swiss Guard at the palace fired and were consequently / subsequently massacred. Six hundred died. The mob attacked royal symbols throughout Paris. The deputies, terrified, decided to rubber-stamp this to try and regain control, so they voted to suspend the monarchy and called a National Convention to draw up a new government. They appointed ministers and acted as if things were normal. The king and his family were locked in prison. In reality, the commune of Paris was in charge, and the Assembly did whatever it was told, even promoting sectional firebrand Georges Danton to Minister of Justice.

Fear, anger, hate. The commune was exhibiting all three as it unleashed itself on those it blamed for the war's failure. Lafayette fled abroad before he could be killed, but the commune created a tribunal to try those suspected of opposition, guillotining those found guilty with no evidence or argument. Just about any doubt could get you killed. Refractories who hadn't fled were attacked. Then the commune issued passports and banned people from leaving Paris without permission. The whole atmosphere in Paris had become one of violent paranoia. Traitors were seen everywhere. Arrests were made everywhere, with a search of every property to find them.

Marat wasn't a new voice in Paris. A hateful, possibly deranged polemicist and journalist, he had been writing for a while. But the people were scared and paranoid and listened to

142

what he preached, and what he preached was the murder of traitors, prisoners and everyone opposed to or failing France.

The Assembly now tried to wrestle power back from the commune, and the two struggled, with the latter inviting Marat into power. On September 2nd, news reached Paris that the Prussians had passed the last fortress before Paris, and everyone assumed a revenging army would arrive any day. People panicked, a powder keg of fear exploded, and sans culottes began massacring prisoners, who they believed were traitors about to be freed by Prussia to take revenge. The commune reacted to the massacres by pointing them in a more efficient, but no less murderous, direction. Prisons were emptied, ad hoc tribunals rushed through and over a thousand people killed. The commune asked the provinces to follow suit. Priests, royal hangers-on, politicians and more traditional criminals were hacked apart.

For the sans culottes, this freed them. No longer worried about enemies in the rear, units of them marched to fight the invaders. Tens of thousands of citizen soldiers formed into an army, aided in a major way by young, trained and hungry gunners of a low enough rank to be considered by the paranoid as truly revolutionary and not masquerading nobles. At Valmy on September 20th the enthusiasm and quantity of these troops halted the Prussian advance. Those who witnessed the charge of the patriots knew a new era had begun. Brunswick had to pull

143

his army back rather than try again, and the hopes of Louis XVI went with him.

The Death of the King

Prussia started peace talks, and promptly stopped and retreated because of the news from Paris. The National Convention met, after elections on August 27th which allowed all men but servants and the unemployed to vote. Members of the Constituent Assembly therefore return to our story, as members of the National Convention. The first thing it did was announce France's transformation into a republic. As before, the deputies were mostly lawyers and other professionals, but the majority were young and opposed to the king and his vetoes. The declaration of a republic was inevitable: the Paris commune and mob demanded nothing less. Monarchy ended on September 21st, 1792. Their armies kept pressing, and the last few months of the year saw highs: advances into Nice, Savoy, the Rhineland and, thanks to Demouriez swamping the Austrians at Jemappes, Brussels and Antwerp.

There was the question of what do to with former king Louis XVI. The 'Girondins' (a faction of less radical Jacobins) wanted to keep him a hostage. Both the Montagnards (a faction of more radical Jacobins named 'mountain' because they sat high up in the Assembly) and the commune wanted him tried and executed. When the *armoire de fer* (a chest) was found in the

144

Tuileries filled with documents showing Louis' flirtation with counter revolution, opinion hardened. Robespierre and others now joined the call. The Convention decided to try the former king in front of their own Convention, and on December 11th he first appeared in 'court'. A sort of trial occurred. The old king was defended by a loyal old servant, the former lawyer and minister Malesherbes. He knew it was an impossible job that would see hm executed as well as the king, but he did it anyway.

Louis was always going to be found guilty because, as Robespierre pointed out, an innocent verdict would wreck the claims of the revolution. So he was found guilty, and deputies argued over the punishment. A call to ask the people was rejected over fear that asking the populace would divide them once more. So the convention itself voted on whether to execute Louis, and many voted yes out of fear of the sans culottes rioting. 361 voted yes to execute, 288 voted no, and 72 tried to extemporise. Consequently, on January 21st, 1793, at the Place de la Concorde, Louis XVI of France was beheaded. Later on, Malesherbes was too.

A financial crisis had turned into a constitutional revolution, which in turn fell under the control of a Parisian grass roots movement that was turned to extremes by the fear of war, bringing a republic and the death of the king. The point of no return hadn't been passed so much as set on fire. Around

Europe, the enemies of France became hardened. Within France, the opponents of the regime knew they might not have long to live.

CRIB

- A new constitution is created, and it includes the king and a veto. The resulting Legislative Assembly opens, dominated by the bourgeoisie.

- The Assembly proposes laws attacking émigrés and priests who won't swear the oath; Louis vetoes them.

- Many in France now want war with Austria and others. Some want to prevent an invasion and defend the borders, others want a war to flush out counter-revolutionary Frenchmen and unite the people, and even the king wants a war because he wants to be saved.

- Consequently, France declares war on Austria.

- The war goes badly, and everyone in France grows more extreme. A mob of people break into the royal family's home and abuse them.

- Enemy armies have success, close on Paris and an enemy general issues a threat to destroy the capital if the king is harmed. All this does is trigger a riot and a massacre of prisoners and the king's guards.

- The French manage to win a victory at Valmy and push the invaders back.
- Growing ever more extreme, fuelled by mob violence, the deputies of France decide to create a regime which does not have a king. The republicans then prosecute and execute Louis XVI.

8: War Within / War Without

The International War

Few things upset a king (or emperor) like seeing a fellow king beheaded by his own population when your own population is getting restless. It rather sets a bad precedent. The consequence of Louis' death was to bring home to the leaders of Europe how stunningly serious this actually was, and the execution was underlined in very thick font by the military situation. For several years of the French Revolution the deputies had looked like they were posturing: attack us and we'll export our freedom to your enemy state. This hadn't seemed much of a threat when the officer corps of the French army was mostly in exile, and at the start of the war the French army had been battered.

But then things changed in one of the most gloriously surprising instances of national response. Civilian volunteers in their thousands went to the front line, formed into an army under Dumouriez and halted the Prussian advance on Paris before the French commander realised what he had and marched this force, cheering "Vive la Nation" and using tactics of charging madly into now outnumbered opponents, into Belgium and the Austrian Netherlands. Dumouriez didn't just have numbers: a lot of clever and able military men were promoted from the lower ranks up into command. Suddenly ability could get you a position, and there were many able lower rankers, particularly in an artillery wing that had never been trendy for nobles.

Louis XVI hadn't ever had the money to interfere in the Austrian / Low Countries struggle, and Dumouriez's rag-tag revolutionaries conquered it quickly. Then other French commanders pushed into Savoy and Nice. In a few months the curio, the viral video of the French revolution killed a king and started occupying neighbouring states, with a self-styled desire to challenge the entire European social and political order. It was incendiary.

Europe is a big place, and the western events weren't happening on their own. The partition of Poland had exploded into a rebellion, with Polish forces fighting Russia, and so Prussia focused on gaining land in eastern Europe in that chaos rather than supporting Austria in the west. With Prussia pulled east and Austria slow, France charged on. The deputies of France now experienced a surge of elation, from the lows of military failure to the highs of thinking they were right, and the Convention announced that "in the name of the French Nation … it will accord fraternity and help to all peoples who wish to recover their liberty." That meant allowing French generals to impose every revolutionary decision taken in France on the 'freed' territory of their conquests. It was, in one way, a declaration of war on Europe. Anyone with privilege, feudal rights, monarchical power—an entire social order—was

149

threatened. But there was a twist: the deputies declared that nations being helped would have to pay for that help. If the French marched in, your money was going to march back out.

This wasn't entirely naked land-grabbing from a nation which had banned expansionist war a few years before. Over the centuries, the French borders had moved, and there were Francophile elements in these regions. The idea of France's 'natural borders', i.e. the sea, the Rhine, the Alps and the Pyrenees, weren't outlandish and saw supporters within the 'foreign' states. Admittedly, many Belgians who welcomed France were expecting to have their own Belgian nation set up with their own Convention and weren't thrilled when deputies in France argued Belgium should be part of France with representatives in their Convention. And, of course, you had Dumouriez, who was indeed after a naked land grab and favoured a country for himself, a king-making role in France, or whatever he could get.

People in the non-Austrian Netherlands, both for and against Austria / France / Independence, weren't slow to realise that they were included in this 'natural border' region. Nor were the British slow to react to continental events. You might remember how, famously, the British declared war in World War One because of a promise to defend Belgium. Well, that story is a bit more complex than that, but suffice to say even by this point Britain had a policy of making sure Belgium and Holland, with whom they closely traded, remained not French at all, and suddenly here was France invading and incorporating. Belgium was conquered. The Dutch Republic might be next. Britain, ready to send money (if not always troops) to affect the balance of power in Europe, readied a response. The French deputies, carried away by glee and bloodshed, declared war on Britain, the Dutch Republic and then Spain, while Danton literally called for war on the whole of Europe. Dubious staged votes were held, France expanded, and Dumouriez marched into the Dutch Republic.

You might be sat at home wondering whether taking on a huge number of countries at the same time with a young army and blood-crazed politicians was a good idea, and you've probably concluded it wasn't. You're right, because by early 1793, Prussia and Austria had settled the Polish issue (at Poland's expense) and turned back to France, and their armies attacked once more. This time, Dumouriez was hammered in battle at Neerwinden. Furthermore, Britain was doing what it did best in these things: it used money and diplomacy to tie the opponents of France in a big coalition against the revolutionaries. Even Russia, not known for its proximity to France, joined the British invitation.

French forces were pushed out of the Rhineland, and Dumouriez reacted to defeat by ordering his men to march, not east, but west, where he planned to conquer Paris and free the old king's son. His troops refused, so he went east and joined the Austrians. You can imagine how that fuelled the paranoia in the French capital, and a Committee of Public Safety was created. Robespierre demanded anyone asking for peace should be guillotined. Another general replaced Dumouriez, but Dampierre was killed and the next man up—Custine—was guillotined by his own side. As the nation collapsed into civil war, a term not often used in books on the French Revolution but entirely accurate, enemy troops pushed on. Belgium fell, Mainz fell, the Spanish border fell, even Toulon, a vast naval port, fell to the British. But that was the problem. These were all in a ring around France, not the core. No enemy force went to Paris, no one pushed deep in. The coalition had no leader, no formal organisation. Everyone pushed France back within its borders and waited for it to collapse, allowing the revolutionaries to regroup and fight their battles. This inability to only get half together would bedevil the enemy cause right the way down to the end of the Napoleonic Wars.

The French re-organised their forces, and this involved executing some generals and finding more republican ones. A commander called Houchard had the Army of the North, and he used a combination of old regime professionalism and the mass of conscript numbers to push the coalition back. But he was also guillotined by his own side, accused of not following up his victory quickly enough. Austria was looking safer for commanders.

Their next French hero was Jourdan, a military man who worked closely with Carnot, a Committee of Public Safety man, and they brought hundreds of thousands of men into the military. Yes, the call for 300,000 conscripts in February 1793 caused vast rebellion in France, including the Vendée War explained below, but soon France had over 700,000 troops, a historical first.

What Happens Next

The next pages will focus on events in France in the form of the Civil War and the Terror, so we'll continue with the outside war for a bit in this chapter.

Carnot and the Convention changed the face of global war. For the first time in history, a nation called for the *'levée en masse'*, the mobilisation of everyone and every horse, total war against their enemies. Everyone was to be in the army or in service to the war effort. By the middle of 1794, France had the largest force in European history. To achieve this, France reformatted the armed forces. They mixed trained troops with new troops to produce a functioning force and equalised all pay and equipment and reformed tactics. The era of small forces of highly trained soldiers able to make complex manoeuvres, the 'Great' part in Frederick the Great, turned into a vast civilian force charging en masse in wave after wave. The officer corps was filled by the promotion of people good enough, and it was said every soldier potentially had a general's baton in their knapsack. Certainly, a young artilleryman called Napoleon Bonaparte had, and his skill at retaking Toulon was the start of a rise we'll encounter again in this book.

By mid-1794 the French had started winning again, the Committee of Public Safety having made some of the most effective and ruthless organisational decisions you'll ever read about (we return to its origins below). Aided by more chaos in Poland, the tide turned, and France had the upper hand. While the rebellion of the Polish against their conquerors isn't going to be covered in depth here, you will want to know that the rebels wore tricolour cockades, sang the Marseillaise and were considered by themselves and their enemies as International Jacobins. The example of the revolution had spread, even if France couldn't be persuaded to launch a full-scale support mission. Poland was wiped off the map.

France produced more soldiers, equipment and patriotic materials to send to the front than their rivals, but they also sent 67 generals back home that year after executing them.

Austria, bloodied and battered, now withdrew. In theory the war had turned, but deputies were afraid of disbanding the armies and flooding France with soldiers who would destabilise. Unfortunately, neither could French finances support the armies. The solution was to invade once again—in theory to defend revolution, but in practice to gain gold and glory. The motives behind these wars had thus changed before Napleon arrived to more nakedly seek treasure and fame. France took Belgium, the Austrian Netherlands and started on the Dutch Republic. The ruler of the latter, William V, fled from 'patriots' as his realm rebelled, and France marched in to establish a new Batavian Republic entirely subject to French rule, which it began to loot.

Pressure from the reborn French broke the coalition. Prussia quit, doing a deal that gave France the left bank of the Rhine and her the right. The left was incorporated and plundered. Spain did better, negotiating peace in fear of suffering their own uprising. Austria and Britain considered peace, the former needing loans from the latter, but France offered no concessions.

The deputies of 1792 had started a war to both end the threat of external enemies, and to expose and crush their internal enemies. They had gone further, more extreme, than even they had planned, turning a whole continent's ruling class against them. The French Revolutionary Wars would be fought until 1797 and kill a huge number of people. During this a leader would rise, Napoleon, who would embroil Europe in war for even longer. And while this happened, France was burning inside.

The Vendée and Civil War

That is the story of the international war, but during the same period the deputies and sans culottes of France would have to deal with the other part of their plan: they would fight a civil war against their internal enemies. This book has concentrated on events in Paris, and now it will open up to the provinces. But that focus comes into even starker contrast now because the mob of Paris, the self-aware, self-declared 'sans culottes', were the ones directing the revolution now, and the deputies in the Convention knew it. These newly returned and arrived representatives tried to pass a law ending the Paris commune, but it was totally ignored on the streets. The reliable National Guard units had been sent to the front to fight, and the Parisian unit was filled with sans culottes. The entire revolutionary government was threatened by, and at the whim of, the sans culottes. A power struggle now began between the deputies and the Parisians.

A loose group of deputies called the Girondins were the head of the opposition. At the start of the republican revolt Robespierre and other right wingers had tried to have the Girondins arrested, in which case they'd have certainly been massacred. This gave a personal edge to their opposition to Robespierre, who they felt wanted to seize power. They weren't really a party in the way Robespierre and his backers were, and

156

could never mobilise enough support, unlike the mass of Jacobins. Nevertheless, they were able to co-ordinate enough to propose laws, like one creating an armed force sent from the provinces to guard the Convention from the mob.

The Convention was now clearly split by factions. The Montagnards sat high up on one side, the Girondons on the other, and the mass of deputies who sat between them became known as The Plain. The Girondins made speeches against the Montagnards and attacked Marat, who in turn called for massacres and a dictator. The Montagnards accused the Girondins of wanting to put a relative of the king on a constitutional throne; the Girondins said the massacres dishonoured the nation. The Montagnards expelled Girondins from the Jacobin club, as they did anyone less extreme.

Just when the struggle in France seemed to have turned into deputies in a chamber, the people of Paris exerted themselves. Prices were rising, money was becoming scarce as war drained the nation and disrupted production and supply of goods. The sans culottes demanded the Convention apply maximum prices, and in a rare show of unity the Convention demurred. But Marat had been demanding hoarders be guillotined, and the sans culottes rioted. The deputies were once more afraid of the mob.

Tensions were high when the deputies again did something that cleaved France into factions. The war was straining supply, and a call had gone out for more men. After all, the hordes of

157

patriots had seemed to offer a solution. A levy of 300,000 men was called, conscripted by the drawing of lots if necessary. Every region of France was given a quota.

This was unpopular on a nuclear level. There were angry reactions across France, but in the Vendée, on the west coast, the many divisions of the revolution had created such upset and friction that the levy was the last straw. Lower class citizens saw the local bourgeoisie claim exemptions from the front, exile popular priests, invest in church land and support killing the king. They hated it. Initial violent reaction against conscription turned into a vast open rebellion against the centre, Paris, deputies, local profiteers and immunities. It became a huge civil war of rebels versus revolutionaries. There were rebellions across France, and local rebels fought National Guard and other forces, but in the Vendée rebels stormed towns and turned an entire region 'white', as the royalist rebels took on the royal symbols. This wasn't a class war, as the whites were drawn from all levels of society. It was a civil war.

The Committee of Public Safety

In Paris, news of France's provincial wobbles came in and mixed with bad news from the front. The Girondins had identified themselves with Dumouriez, reflecting badly. At a low ebb of the war, as their whole world seemed to be collapsing, a group among both the deputies and the sans culottes reacted with fear and paranoia and were pushed, as humans tend to be, into extreme reactions. They called for the death of opponents, the sacking of deputies, a revolutionary tribunal to judge and execute traitors. The Convention leaned this way, and the tribunal was created. So were the 'representatives on mission', which were deputies who were to travel to all the localities in France, with guillotines if needed, to organise the crushing of rebellion.

That wasn't enough for some, and extremists in Paris called for a mob uprising to arrest the Girondins and others deemed not patriotic enough. At this point the commune demurred from agreeing and the mob rising was aborted, but the idea was there. Girondon supporters were harassed.

The effect on the Girondins was terrible. They took their eye off the Convention and sank into paranoia about attacks on themselves, which meant the Montagnards practically took over: their supporters went en mission, their laws created watch committees to spy on everyone, and their idea for a smaller, stronger central body to conduct government and war led to the creation of the twenty-five-man Committee of Public Safety, which became a nine-man body when it started on April 7th, 1793. Robespierre, the man most associated with it, rejected joining at this point as he didn't think it of much consequence. Robespierre was many things, and one of them was wrong.

The Revolutionary Tribunal became the source of open war between deputies. The Montagnards created it to try opponents, but the Girondins, acting without clear thought, proposed a law removing the deputies' protection from it, which the Montagnards passed so they could attack the Girondins. First, the Girondins managed to send Marat to it. The people of Paris were livid that their favourite was in danger and threatened the Convention. Probably because of this, the Tribunal found Marat innocent and the sans culottes took this as a sign his policy was approved: kill hoarders, impose price controls. The Montagnard deputies were pulled along by the sans culottes mobbing the Convention and finally agreed to price controls. Their own lives in danger, the Girondins called for the Convention to move to Versailles to avoid mob pressure, a call which sounds as incendiary two centuries later as it did then.

The Civil War Spreads

Now the Vendée was joined in rebellion, not just by rural localities, but by major cities. No less than the home of the revolutionary anthem, Marseille, was first. Local Jacobins had copied those in Paris with tribunals and attacks on the rich, but a major port so disrupted by war found a huge number of people desiring peace and normality, and those against the changes coming from Paris rebelled in turn, organised a committee and rose. The Jacobins and the Representative en Mission had to flee. The watchword was 'Federalism', opposition to the centre and the Republic. With news of Marseille's counter revolution spreading, combined with the zealotry of local Jacobins, a string of provinces and cities rejected the revolution and rebelled. Even Lyon, second after Paris in importance, turned. Back in the Vendée, tens of thousands of armed militiamen kept the white cause expanding.

There were many reasons for supporting the revolution, and likewise for opposing it. A simple rule is that the more you were negatively affected by the events (losing your land, your venal offices, your position as a priest, your religion) the more likely you were to rebel against revolution, and the more you profited (buying church land, promotions, new political voice) the more likely you were to support it.

Back in Paris, the Montagnards suddenly felt the consequence of sending many of their members into the provinces: there were less of them to outvote the Girondins. Indeed, the Girondins grew in popularity as opposition to the tribunal and other extreme action coalesced around them. They knew there were plots against them, so they bound together and managed to get a 'Commission of Twelve' created to investigate and act against mob action in Paris. Plans were made for a backup Convention away from Paris, arrests were called for, and the Girondins made clear they might bring in troops and support from the provinces.

The enemies of the Girondins acted in several ways, including begging the Girondins to stop provoking Paris and try and get everything working again: there was a war being fought, a threat of invasion to repel, this was not a time for civil war. The Girondins refused. It became clear to the Montagnards that it was time to purge the Convention or lose it entirely. So, the Montagnards got a vote passed ending the Commission of Twelve and freeing any prisoners not yet executed. There was once again a mob rising, but the leaders of the street couldn't decide on whether to end the Girondin's careers or just shock them into passivity. That day ended with threats but no purge. What caused clarity was news of Lyon's betrayal arriving, which looked like a Girondin plot to bring support from the provinces. Now the sans culottes rose, allied with the thousands of National Guard, and surrounded the Convention. They arrested twenty-nine deputies. The rest, realising the mob would erase the Convention if they did not bow, voted approval. Many of the Plain refused to vote, and this would haunt them.

The Girondins never had a programme like a modern political party. They were a loose alliance of deputies who opposed the Convention acting up to the whims of the Paris mob. The Montagnards were the opposite, people who responded in fear and tried to come to terms with the Parisians and keep the Convention in existence. The Montagnards only agreed to purge the Girondins when it looked like the entire system of representative deputies was going to fall to the sans culottes. This was not a coup or a change of government. This was not Robespierre's extreme calls for purity and Terror. This was a struggle of ideas and powers and pragmatism between rival politicians who all feared what the Parisians would enforce. The Montagnards took a long time to decide on a purge and resisted it for a long while. They only did so in the end out of fear.

Assassins

Bordeaux, home of the Girondins, rebelled hard, and called on rebellious departments of France to send troops for a march on Paris to restore order. Soldiers were raised, counter-revolutionary tribunals were created, Jacobins were killed, war was fought. Thousand died. But the counter revolutionaries were divided. Few sought to reverse the revolution and bring the king back; instead they wanted an end to Parisian mob domination and a return to deputies representing the whole nation. An end to the extremes of the war: conscription and battles. Those who did want the return of the king fell out with those aiming simply for a return to 1791. In fact, the rebel forces included very few royalists, and even fewer people who wanted to march and fight the capital. Yes, there were thousands of rebel soldiers, but they didn't want to leave their homes / home regions. Paris sat safely, only harassed, sending representatives out to wage war.

The Montagnards now moved to conciliate. They ordered émigré land to be sold in small lots of the sort peasants could afford. They ordered a new constitution with universal manhood suffrage, and all documents and compensation relating to the end of feudal rights were literally burned. But not everyone was trying to bring peace. Marat was still screaming about murder, and a rebel woman from Caen called Charlotte Corday confronted him as he bathed and stabbed him to death. A murdered Montagnard? The reaction was fear once more, paranoia, the sense of the whole world collapsing around the deputies. Now Robespierre stepped forward, believing the Committee of Public Safety could be used to secure his revolution. These were extreme times and people believed extreme action was needed. Brutality was required to bring security. When the new Constitution was approved and put into practice, Robespierre had it suspended to deal with the current emergency.

CRIB

- The war swings back and forth, and the French prove as dangerous to their commanders as the enemy, executing dozens who 'underperform'.

- When France has success, they advance into neighbouring lands and a call goes out to conquer the 'natural borders' and export the changes of the revolution into them. France declares war on ever more nations.

- The war begins to spiral out of control. In response, France turns itself into the first nation to wage Total War by calling for the *levée en masse*, putting everyone to work in the war effort. Their armies, carrying out patriotism-fuelled mass advances, change warfare.

- Meanwhile, a combination of conscription, treatment of priests and hostility to the centre causes vast areas of France to explode into armed opposition, chief of all the Vendée. The Parisian deputies now fight a civil war. Deputies called 'Representatives en Mission' are sent to crush them.

- In Paris, the government is being pushed to extremes, working from fear and exhaustion. To speed up their response, a Committee of Public Safety is created to centralise actions.

- The capital has an atmosphere of massive paranoia, with spies hunting down opposition. The Revolutionary Tribunal tries the accused on the basis of no evidence and the mob are making demands of the deputies. When Charlotte Corday kills Marat, a journalist openly calling for the death of thousands, fear grows.

- A new constitution is created but suspended because of the 'emergency' of the wars.

9: The Terror

It was now later 1793. For a deputy in Paris, the world seemed about to end. The external war was going badly with enemy troops on the fringes of French soil, while the internal war saw cities and provinces dropping out of central control. Things weren't much better in Paris itself, with Charlotte Corday triggering the fear that assassins where everywhere, while lawmakers needed to keep the Paris mob on side. People were terrified and emotions were hyped up.

In times of chaos and panic, extreme actions can easily happen. The members of the Committee of Public Safety had ensured that the new constitution was suspended, and they appealed to the Convention (who hadn't yet been replaced) to make the CPS the government of France, so that they might right these issues. Given what comes next it might be surprising to know that the Convention refused, so the Committee was never France's official full-time government even if it went on to act in exactly that way and bring in extraordinary measures. For the Committee would decide on a regime which nakedly used Terror as a weapon.

Carnot now joined the Committee and set about transforming the war. At first it seemed like the internal conflict was swinging back the way of Paris and the centre: the Representatives en Mission and their National Guard forces

167

won back a string of towns and cities, and while they didn't quite have the guillotines on wheels a deputy had demanded, they were not conciliatory to the rebels. Executions were common. But the paranoia was tweaked by Toulon. Rebels fleeing from the Representatives reached Toulon, which was anti the Parisian mob rather than anti the whole of the revolution. But when the British offered this important naval base protection if they came out in favour of a new king, a bitter argument ended with just that happening. British ships sailed in.

Once again, Paris was frightened. Marat might have gone, but the city was filled with writers who wanted that fame and pushed a brutal agenda to get it. They wanted enemies, hoarders, spies, rebels and traitors rooted out and guillotined. The answer, they believed, lay in a reign of Terror against the enemy. Some deputies joined in and worked to persuade the whole Jacobin movement to accept it. More shortages and supply issues caused another mob gathering on September 4th, and the extremists used this to pressure the Convention into 'applying the law', which meant sending armies into the countryside to kill hoarders and bring back food. It also caused the Revolutionary Tribunal to be sped up, demanding that everyone loyal should be armed, that enemies be crushed. The Convention acquiesced.

In fact, the Convention went into overdrive to promote Terror. It passed a new law on September 17, the Law of Suspect, whose wording basically allowed for literally anyone to be arrested and charged. The situation became so bad that if you didn't refer to each other as 'citizens' you might get imprisoned. A General Maximum Law took over the setting of prices on goods.

Even now, Robespierre was trying to keep some sense of control and common sense. He tried to stop both the Girondins and the former queen, Marie Antoinette, from being put on trial. Other leading figures were arrested. Then, finally, the members of the Committee of Public Safety managed to get the power of the nation routed through them and not the Convention, which would remain officially in charge and with oversight. In practice, Revolutionary Government and the implementation of Terror fell to the men of the Committee of Public Safety.

When people think of revolutions going wrong, of bloody bad things, this is what they imagine. The Committee of Public Safety ran a campaign of deliberate, explicitly named Terror in Paris and across France which killed over 15,000 in just nine months. Robespierre became a convert. Marie Antoinette went to the blade, as did the Girondins, ex-nobles, leaders of the early revolution deemed not extreme enough and many others. Practically anyone could fall foul. The most fatalities came from rebel areas now recaptured, with so many killed in such a short time they had to be shot with bullets (as in Toulon when

Napoleon retook it), or just huddled in groups and fired with cannons as in Lyon, or even tied up and sunk in boats (Nantes).

Representatives and their 'Revolutionary Armies' of terrorist sans culottes smashed the rebels back, and in the Vendée multiple Committee armies defeated the disorganised Whites, who failed in an attempt to link with the British and were slaughtered. Then the Committee's troops set the area ablaze in punishment. Over two hundred thousand people might have died. An even greater number were arrested under the Law of Suspects: across France, half a million, with thousands dying in prison from mistreatment. But less than ten per cent were old nobles, and the same was true of priests: the Terror was not an erasure of rich by poor. It was a civil war.

Other things sprung from Terror. Priests weren't a target, but republican deputies could certainly pursue new ideas and turn against the old, and in October a former priest called Fouché published an appeal to a new kind of religion: all 'cults' were to be considered equal, but none were to be state run or public except a universal kind of morality. Naturally, such a reform went alongside removing the traces of the old religion, and these ideas would get back to Paris and begin a movement known as dechristianization, which in turn spread out. The Paris Commune took the idea up wholeheartedly, as did the Committee. The calendar of France was erased, the year of Christ's birth no longer deemed relevant, and the Revolutionary

Calendar was numbered from the start of the Republic on September 22nd, 1792. Sunday vanished, and the Representatives encouraged a war against the Church: smashing churches, taking bells, defrocking priests and executing those refractories who would not be flee. The Jacobins tried to erase the Christian Church, and Robespierre, who disliked Christianisation, tried to introduce a new religion celebrating reason and wisdom, worshipping Liberty and the Supreme Being. Robespierre was worried. He believed people needed religion, and had tried to stop his revolutionaries making more enemies still. He found he could not, so worked on taking greater control of the Terror he had lost control of.

A decree outlined what form the 'Revolutionary Government' would take. The Convention were at the top with no power, and the Committee centralised power to an extent not seen before: Representatives were now banned from freelancing their way round the rules. Everyone was ordered to do what the Committee told them, and the Law of 14 Frimaire structured power and oversight down from the Committee through National Agents, past Representatives to local councils. All previous revolutionary structures in France had separate powers, and they spread them down and out to the localities. The Committee scooped it all up for themselves.

It worked. The chaos and independence of forces outside Paris slowed. Dechristianization stopped, the Revolutionary Armies ended their slaughter. The Terror continued, but under central direction. Perhaps nowhere was this as clear as in the price controls the Committee set for French goods. 1790 was the baseline, with wages set at 150% of the rate in that year and thirty-nine products at 133%.

However, it wasn't just murder. Robespierre and his fellows were also passing some of the most progressive legislation yet seen, like the Bocquier Law of compulsory but free state education for all children aged six to thirteen, although this was partly to indoctrinate them all. The state now looked after homeless children, and people born outside marriage received the inheritance rights of everyone else. The metric system of weights and measurements came in, and money was spent on reducing poverty—although, again, that was double edged as the money came from the property of the dead.

There was opposition to the Terror, of course there was, but it was hard to vocalise as it would have seen you executed. The Terrorists were at their strongest when the wars had been going wrong, when they argued that extraordinary times meant extraordinary responses, when it seemed that maybe, just maybe, executing traitors would save the rest of the population. But by the end of 1794 the tide had turned. The wars within and without were going the way of the centre, and people in Paris began to wonder if Terror could be slowed, stopped, if a better government could emerge. Deputies tried to alter the makeup of the Committee to remove extremism.

Now the Terrorists turned on themselves. Some wanted to go further or just to carry on, others wanted to step back. Robespierre himself tried to create a body to investigate abuses, while Representatives rushed back to defend themselves against accusations of excess. Groups formed, factions argued, with names like Indulgents and Hérbertists. Robespierre and his loyalists decided it was time to purge themselves of trouble makers, and the extreme leaders of the Revolutionary Armies and their supporters fell victim to a plot. They were accused of faking food shortages, massacring prisoners and other abuses which a few months previously had gone full steam ahead. They were arrested and taken to the guillotine, and the people of Paris…

…did not act. The men most in tune with the voice of the mob found the sans culottes were out of energy. The Terror had robbed them of vigour, they were exhausted, and as the Revolutionary Armies were disbanded their leaders and friends, now called Hérbertists, were executed without a rising. But there was to be no peace. The rest of the Terrorists would soon fall; the infighting would destroy them all. Robespierre appears to have completed a move into madness, having finally decided to execute his colleague and friend, Danton.

The Republic of Virtue

To be honest, 'The Republic of Virtue' sounds suspiciously awful two centuries later. While people throughout Paris began to ask where the was Terror going, where would it end, Robespierre was formulating a new idealistic and terrible state of life. It's easy to think of Robespierre, at this point the most powerful individual in the whole of France, as a monster, as crazed. In reality, he is a perfect microcosm of the early half of the revolution: a man once of noble and great ideas (he wanted the death penalty banned) who was driven to extremes through fear, war and circumstance, and who in those extremes lost contact with morality yet thought he *was* morality and went into madness. Robespeirre announced where the Terror would end: a Republic of Virtue.

What did virtue mean? Robespierre defined it as a love of your homeland and its laws, of putting those laws above you and giving selfless service to the nation. Virtue must be the first and main thing you strive for. He was quite specific that the enemy of virtue is counter revolution, and that all who opposed it, all who weren't virtuous, must be corrected or erased. Robespierre didn't invent this; he was heavily influenced by the work of Rousseau, who argued that people were naturally good but corrupted by poverty and brutal elites and that a virtuous world could be created. Robespierre identified with this so much he thought he was the bringer of perfect virtue and that blood was a necessary vehicle.

Robespierre, however, was not well. That isn't a snide joke about his mental state; he was literally so beyond the limit of his nerves he had to take a month-long step back from public life. When he returned, he had decided to remove more of his fellow deputies. This time the Indulgents, who had opposed the Herbertists, were arrested, as was a leading voice of (relative) sense, Danton. No one knows what words were exchanged when Robespierre and Danton had a private meeting, but a trial and execution followed soon after. The thing is, Danton and the Indulgents hadn't done anything obvious that would doom them. They weren't campaigning for the return of the king, they weren't like the Herbertists organising a rising. They were executed simply because they might have opposed Robespierre, and this is what the Republic of Virtue was about: not guilt of crimes, but a failure to appear morally upstanding enough. Furthermore, the answer to a lack of virtue was execution. Provincial courts were closed to funnel alleged traitors through the Parisian Revolutionary Tribunal, and that was altered so it could only decide innocence or death. Mostly death. The definition was so wide, the process so focused on execution that the numbers killed by the state rose sharply after a decline. Now the percentage of nobles and priests killed increased.

Robespierre continued to centralise power around himself. He organised the Committee to take control of the Paris Commune, but this neutered it further. When he published wage controls which gave many sans culottes pay cuts, the sections and commune could not argue back. Hold that thought, because it becomes very important in the next chapter.

What was the Terror? It executed eighty-four generals, sixty-seven of 749 convention deputies, it saw a man killed for repeating a line in a seventeenth century play praising the king while they were stood queuing, but was very diverse. Seven departments had no Terror executions at all, but in rebel areas like Vendée, ten to fifteen per cent of the whole population ended up massacred. Ninety per cent of Terror deaths in just twenty of the departments. This wasn't a jack-booted totalitarian state with no opposition—in fact, opposition was everywhere in an atmosphere where everything was heightened, extremes on both sides—but it was a state where that opposition could have you executed the next day, and did so.

Thermidor

There is no better sign of someone losing touch with reality than starting a new cult, and people in Paris knew it. Deputies began to wonder if Robespierre wanted to be king, and even those who had worked with him, even important members of the Committee became afraid for their lives. Furthermore, the war was once again going well. The Terror didn't seem necessary anymore. As a result, a huge quantity turned against Robespierre and looked for their chance to free themselves of him. The first step was sneaking through a law which protected deputies from the new laws. When this passed, they started to organise.

Robespierre was well aware of this, and he attempted to purge himself of enemies he considered lacking sufficient virtue. But his enemies were too numerous, organised, and close to him, and they refused. Consequently, Robespierre stopped appearing in the Convention and the Committee and gave his speeches to the rapt audience of the Jacobin club. Such an action appeared to be the work of a man preparing his own seizure of power.

But how did you stop a conflagration like the Terror? No one rushed to kill anyone else. Then Robespierre disappeared for another month of mental strain, and reappeared shouting angry accusations at his fellows. He appeared in the Convention and declared open warfare on it, and the Committee itself. Everyone knew it was kill or be killed.

Arguments, speeches, movement: there was a rush around, before the deputies of the Convention proposed, voted on and approved the arrest of Robespierre and his devotees. It passed. Robespierre was taken to a cell. He had overestimated his power, and he had alienated everyone who might support him. Even the sans culottes and the sections and commune of Paris

177

did not act, because in his centralising fury Robespierre had broken their ability and will to act, and his wage controls had annoyed them further. He tried to summon the mob to protect him, but they did not come, and the revolution passed a corner. Terror had broken the streets of Paris and the revolution could continue free of the mob.

Imprisoned, Robespierre tried to shoot himself but only shattered his jaw. He was dragged, in agony, to a guillotine and beheaded like so many before. Eighty of his supporters followed. This happened in a month called Thermidor, and the process took that name.

The Convention asserted itself. The membership rules of the committee and other bodies were changed to prevent people gaining power, and a host of Terrorist laws were repealed. Evidence was now needed to execute, and the Terror collapsed. The number of executions fell dramatically and law as we might recognise it returned. Instead of massacring prison populations, the doors were open and people flocked out to safety.

There was a reaction of course. Those harmed by the Terror wanted revenge and fought back against Terrorist supporters. Those who survived wanted to ensure this never happened again. A fashionable rebel group called the Gilded Youth began beating up sans culottes. The reaction against Terror was so strong even the once mighty Jacobin club began to sink under its association with Robespierre. It took the Convention a while, because they wished to move slowly in these new days of release, but they moved to arrest those who had carried out the Terror and finally ordered the closure of the Jacobin clubs. Girondin survivors were released from prison and welcomed back to the Convention, and leading Terrorists were guillotined. The reaction only grew. Jacobins were harassed, Terrorists were expelled, threatened, executed, and their laws stripped away. Revenge, reorganisation, reawakening, a 'White Terror' in which the persecuted struck back hard. A cultural change to a world where your dress and your words would not see you guillotined, where wealth was glorified, were women wore red chokers to mock the former threat of the guillotine. The cult of the Supreme Being was axed, and Christianity allowed back (separate from the state). Even in the Vendée, an amnesty was issued.

There were two final risings by the sans culottes, when a mixture of food shortages and wage issues made the mob wonder whether some parts of the Terrorist plan could come back. But although a few thousand gathered and marched into the Convention calling for price control and the constitution of 1793, it was leaderless, much smaller and without heart. The Convention had loyal National Guards who could repel the people, and did so. The uprisings failed, and the Convention saw quite clearly they were free of the streets, so they purged the Montagnards.

The White Terror saw people on every level, from deputies purging other deputies, to people in villages fighting, revenging themselves on Terrorists. Whereas the Terror had been a form of state rule, this was plain mob justice. As many people were killed in the White Terror as were killed in the Terror itself, as brutally, although often with a more easily understandable justification. Some people managed to pretend they were nothing to do with the Terror and escape. Many did not.

CRIB

- The fear of the deputies, the pressures of the war, the paranoia of the Committee of Public Safety—all lead to the deliberate policy of ruling by Terror: all enemies of the state are to be hunted down and executed. Hundreds of thousands are imprisoned, thousands are executed.

- Marie Antoinette, many deputies and people even making offhand comments about the revolution are executed.

- The man most associated with this is Robespierre, who once called for the abolition of the death penalty.

- A campaign of dechristianisation spreads, born of prejudice. Robespierre tries to counter it with his new religion, the Cult of the Supreme Being.

- Robespierre centralises power even more in the Committee, and in doing so breaks the power of the Parisian mob.

- The Terrorists start to execute more of the deputies, and Robespierre tries to introduce a Republic of Virtue. You can now be executed for 'moral' failings.

- With the war now going well, and with the Terror seemingly able to kill anyone, deputies begin to react and plot a way to end it. When Robespierre appears after a period of illness and threatens basically all the deputies, they swing into action: Thermidor sees the Committee purged, Robespierre and his followers executed and the end of the Terror. The Paris mob is broken and cannot save Robespierre.

- Thousands more die as the victims of the Terror avenge themselves in the White Terror.

10: The Directory

Now the military would begin to replace the mob as the violence behind the revolution, eventually taking over. The Convention turned to the issue of what to do with the constitution. The 1793 document was too associated with the Terrorists, and a new one was needed. Everyone could agree on that. But what? Whispers supporting a system with a royal figurehead ended when the young heir to the throne died and the new heir said he'd go back to the old regime and refused to answer the land question: what would happen to the gains and transfers of the revolution? In a few years, Napoleon would tackle this and keep power as a result. The self-styled Louis XVIII didn't and stayed ignored.

So the deputies needed to enter what was, for the last few years, a rarity: they needed to walk a middle ground which was neither Terrorist or royalist, which honoured the ideals of 1789 and not 1788 or 1793, and to bring a stability the majority wanted after years of chaos. At times good chaos, but chaos nonetheless. The threats from the mob on one side and the royalists on the other had to be negated, and a central position reached which safeguarded the main gains of the revolution, but yet undercut the forces which pushed it, and so bring a peace. Those with the economic stake should be those with the political power.

On August 22nd, 1795, a new constitution was passed. Every man over twenty-one who also paid one of the new taxes could vote, but to be a deputy you had to own a certain amount of property. To keep turnover going and prevent power grabs there would be annual votes, choosing a third of the required deputies each time, and the idea of one chamber was abandoned in favour of the US model of checks and balances on power. So there were now two chambers called 'councils': the Council of Five Hundred would draw up the laws, while the Council of Elders would vote to pass or reject them. The latter didn't have an empty name: to sit in it you had to be over forty and (at some point) married. The top tier of power would be in the Directory, in which five Directors would sit, appointed by the Elders from a list by the Five Hundred. Annual lots would determine who stepped down and was replaced, and you couldn't be a Director and a deputy. Also, it stipulated a considerable period of time for any of this to be changed.

This was all good in theory, but eyebrows were raised when the Convention tacked on a law saying they should comprise two thirds of the first set of deputies. This was unpopular with everyone except the Convention. Even royalists had bought into it and been gearing up for a big election campaign, but no one wanted the tarnished Convention to go on in a new guise. There was a reactionary round of riots and rebellions. One of these was to be very important.

Napoleon

When the results of the election were in, when anger with the returning deputies was highest, when royalists near Paris had to be crushed with troops, the sections of the city gathered for a move. The Convention reacted by trying to ban gatherings and deploying troops to stop them, meaning they had already acted in a more hard-line manner than Louis XVI. National Guards linked with rebels in seven sections and on October 4th a mob of over twenty thousand Parisians closed in on the Convention. To stop them, a deputy called Barras engaged the services of a young artillery commander called Napoleon Bonaparte, and he had positioned cannons. The mob was short of powder and this time had been stripped of artillery, but there was a fight nonetheless between them and soldiers before the Convention won. Napoleon and Barras were ascendant, Paris defeated. Military control was back. The constitution came into effect on October 27th, with five hundred Convention deputies sliding over to the new regime. But one of the new Directors was Barras, an ex-noble and political operator, buoyed by the events of that month. We now also meet Sieyes again, a man who'd been quiet throughout the Terror and who at first turned down the Directory. Only at first. Among those made Directors was Carnot, a man who proved links to Terror could be outweighed by military ability, plus newcomers.

The Directory now continued to try and walk a middle ground, balancing the forces around them. If Jacobins looked ascendant, their newspapers would be curbed and their members harassed, while royalists would be supported (despite this, a reborn Jacobin society, the 'Pantheon Club', grew in strength). When royalists were on the rise, the same happened the other way around. The Paris mob was neutered further by dissolving the sectional assemblies and creating a Parisian Guard loyal to the Directory.

But more than balance was needed. Backup was, support. The events of the last five years had been powered by the weight of the Paris mob. Now the Directory relied on the renewed French army to back them. The rising star of that force was Napoleon.

Cash and Communists

The Assignats collapsed. Gloriously for later writers, I mean that literally, because not only was the value of them almost nothing thanks to vast over-printing and inflation, but the floor of the printing house broke and fell to the room below. The Directory ended their production, but merely replaced them with something that looked suspiciously the same, just resetting many of the problems and only lasting four months. A France which disliked central banks now turned away from national paper money.

There is also a great oddity during this period. A fringe group coalesced who called for the return of the constitution of 1793, Terror and the punishment of the rich. One of the leaders of this was a man called Babeuf, who'd been writing incendiary material for the last few years. What's unusual and has drawn a lot of later ink is that / the fact he was basically the first modern communist in his calls for shared ownership of all property, even if he did call for the worst excesses of the Terror too. Of course, he overstretched and the Directory clamped down on him, and after a failed attempt to seize power he was executed.

1796: Napoleon's Year

By 1796, Austria and France were the mainland powers still at war. France decided offensive was the best form of getting plunder, so aimed to break Austria with a march through Germany in strength, and a distraction force in Northern Italy. The latter weren't meant to make any permanent conquests, but to gain plunder and take enough land to make a worthwhile exchange with Austria for territory around the Rhine. In Germany, Jourdan and Moreau were the French commanders, and facing them was Austrian archduke Charles. The French advanced, Charles blunted them and forced them back, but not before sending his personal soldier over a battlefield to help an injured French general.

Now we come to Italy. Napoleon Bonaparte was given command of the Army of Italy in March 1796, just two days after marrying Joséphine; he was having a good week. It didn't look it though, because although Napoleon had requested this post, there was a key problem: the 'army' of the north was badly equipped, unpaid and deeply unhappy. It was the sort of post the Directory sent Napoleon on to get rid of him so he didn't cause trouble. Now, Napoleon didn't have to fight hard to win these men over, as they knew he was a rising military star and their best chance of glory came with him. These were experienced soldiers who knew a disastrous commander versus a good one, and were thrilled when Napoleon set about transforming the army, getting the needed supplies, enforcing discipline, promising the troops would be paid in cash (once they'd captured it). Napoleon made himself into a character the men could applaud: he re-invigorated the army.

Then it was time to attack. Napoleon benefitted many times in his career from enemies not properly working together, so although Austria and Piedmont had armies in the area, and although they'd have outnumbered Napoleon if they worked together … they didn't, so Napoleon set out to beat them separately. He and his forty thousand men moved quickly, from one to the other, and he pushed Piedmont back and broke their will, forcing a treaty. The Austrians were battered and retreated too, and in less than a month Napoleon was in Lombardy. In

May he crossed the Po, and managed to turn the Battle of Lodi from an unnecessary fight he could have avoided into a glowing reputation builder. Soon he was marching into Milan, and creating a new republican government. The army reacted to Napoleon by embracing him and his success; the soon-to-be emperor believed his own press, too.

Napoleon had to pause to allow the German front to progress, so he went in for a little pressurising, and intimidated gold and treasure from the rest of Italy, passing the sixty million livre mark: his army did indeed get paid. When a new Austrian army appeared, it couldn't have been any easier to beat, as it split itself into two forces and Napoleon defeated them, and then the next army too, showing considerable personal bravery to turn the tide at Arcola. He was exposed to great risk and survived. More battles came, all with successes for Napoleon while Austria made errors, and in mid-January 1797 the French won the battle of Rivoli and advanced into Tyrol. By February, with the surrender of Mantua, Napoleon had conquered North Italy. Even the Pope was paying Napoleon to stay away.

Napoleon saw a further opportunity, and marched on the Austrian capital. Archduke Charles intercepted him but Napoleon forced him back and got / advanced to sixty miles away from Vienna ... when he stopped and offered terms. He'd surprised everyone by getting that close, and even more by stopping. The Austrians were reeling, but Napoleon knew his

188

men were tired and, just as importantly, this was his chance to dictate the peace he wanted, and make his name instead of the Directory's. Discussions started, but while that happened he captured Genoa and turned it into the Ligurian Republic. Parts of Venice also fell before the preliminary Treaty of Leoben was drawn up under Napoleon's direction.

The peace terms were interesting, partly because they were much fairer than Austria was expecting, partly because they carved Venice up and created the Cisalpine Republic, and partly because Napoleon took all the decisions himself and just sent them back to France and the ruling Directory for a rubber-stamp, whereas normally the government would have done it. Napoleon went on, fiddling in Italy at the head of an army and invading Rome. Yet, as he had brought Austria to peace and ended the mainland part of the French Revolutionary Wars, no one back in France was strong enough to stop him. The Peace of Campo Formio of October 18th gave France natural borders, and approved a string of new states under the French banner. When other generals failed to make any dent on Britain (trying to go via an invasion and uprising in Ireland), Napoleon looked even greater. Britain, with no allies left, out of pocket and suffering internal frustrations, sat and simmered. It alone would not meet French demands for peace.

The Embryonic Empire

189

Belgium had experienced several years of being treated like a conquered country, with Paris seizing as much wealth as it could to fund the wars, debts and problems of revolutionary France. When a decision was taken to incorporate Belgium into the French Republic, this exploitation changed into a repeat of history, as deputies who had learned nothing pushed on Belgium exactly the policies which had done so much to divide France, including selling off monasteries and sacking priests. The result was the same, with a Belgian rebellion that had to be crushed. Further north in the Netherlands, a Batavian Republic had been set up, complete with its own Directory, but this wasn't at any peace either and a French-backed general staged a coup. Holland had more freedom than Belgium, but France looked on hungrily. Neither had any chance to resist, and there was little desire to return to the old, equally imperial rulers.

In contrast, the Prince-Bishops of the left bank of the Rhine and their subjects suffered even more. The French wanted 'natural frontiers', so the left bank was split into four departments, but there was no assimilation: the prince-bishops fled and the region was treated as an occupied warzone, with anything of wealth taken for the war effort and the people used to prolong it. The rules of Republican France were not welcomed here, and few people warmed to the devastation. Switzerland was attractive to France to clear the route to Napoleon's Italian conquests, so it was taken over and a constitution was imposed while troops marched through and the nation was used as a bank, albeit just to make withdrawals.

The Directory hadn't meant to conquer Italy, or set up a string of child Republics, until Napoleon marched through at speed, conquering everything. But before this had even finished, Bonaparte, his soldiers, and everyone looking on from Paris had begun asset-stripping the wealthy Italian lands to pay for the war and beyond. A huge amount of art and treasure was shipped back to the awkwardly expanding homeland of 'freedom'.

Coups

Back in France, the political factions jockeyed around for position in the 1797 elections. Although both Jacobins and Royalists still had elements engaged in physical challenges to the Directory, many on both sides were settling in to the idea of winning the 1797 election. Jacobins were well known for their clubs and organisations, but royalists formed their own too, albeit often with foreign money. Indeed the latter still felt public opinion and opportunity was swinging their way again. The self-declared king was still unhelpfully extreme, but was persuaded to at least nod in the direction of concession. The government, by which I mean the ex-Convention deputies and the Directory, also campaigned for themselves.

Voting figures were low. People were burned out, but still the return seemed clear. Most former convention deputies were

191

rejected, and few Jacobins were elected. 182 outward royalists were installed. The Directory, which had worked for a year on a stable power base of ex-Convention deputies, suddenly found all bets off. One even called for the election to be annulled...

This request found support. Barras, and two other Directors in Reubell and La Revelliere, wished to secure their power in the face of a seeming rise in monarchism. The Councils started discussing helping refractory priests and curbing the Directory, so the latter reached out to the generals of France and found support from Napoleon, amongst others who didn't want the wars to have ended only for the kings to return. Using evidence that the new president of the Five Hundred was acting suspiciously (by their definition), the Directory made a move in the direction of Jacobinism and moved troops to the Paris area.

The Councils knew the Directory, now considered to be just three 'Triumvirs', were moving against their attempts at royalism, but they carried on pushing, aiming to build their power over a series of elections until they could bring the king back. But they moved fast, and ended all laws attacking refractories in August 1797. The Directory responded with a military coup, positioning troops in Paris, arresting the opposition part of the Directory and dozens of council deputies, while a handmade body of other deputies gave the approval demanded of them. There was no violent resistance, and the remainder of the councils annulled the royalist part of the

192

election. Replacements were appointed, including two new tame Directors.

The Second Directory

A precedent had been set. The 'Second Directory' would now use the military to overrule any elections they didn't like. However, as they now had a clear power base, the Directory could explode into action. Firstly, they shunted Napoleon out of the way. With the death of a rival general, Napoleon was now the undisputed star of the military, and the Directory weren't keen on having him near. When he dreamt up an attack on Egypt to threaten Britain's empire, the Directory agreed and let him sail to the Middle East. They felt a little safer at night.

Then they 'solved' the financial crisis. Neither Louis XVI, the original deputies or the men of the Terror had preferred bankruptcy to managing the debts which had caused the revolution, but the Directors took pragmatic action and declared a Two Thirds Bankruptcy, in which two thirds of the debt was erased. The tax system was rebuilt, both in terms of what was levied and how it was collected, and indirect taxes returned. Two principles of 1789 had been abandoned.

Attacks on refractories and émigrés began after a lull during the royalist councils. Many had returned to France under the Directory and now had to flee again; many were arrested and executed. The growth of the Jacobins continued, urged on by an attempt to influence the 1798 elections: rising Jacobins might edge out royalists. When 1798's results came in the royalists didn't gain, but Jacobins faced a problem: the Directors had installed a series of checks on the election results which meant they could reject deputies, and they staged a second coup within a year to pack the councils with supporters. The Directory was determined to walk a middle way, with royalists and Jacobins forced to the sides.

The Directors seemed to have home under control, but France's foreign policy went wrong. The Directors and the generals engineered the fall of the Swiss government and the creation of a French allied republic, and the conquest of Rome. The Pope became a prisoner, and died in captivity. For the rest of Europe it became clear that France was a bully, if not a tyrant. Napoleon was marching with speed and efficiency through the Middle East, but who dared oppose France?

Britain reacted to the Middle East threat by dispatching a naval force under Nelson to tackle Napoleon's supply line, and at the Battle of the Nile they thrashed the French fleet. Napoleon was stuck. The Ottomans had also reacted by declaring war on France, and now Naples did too, as did the Russians. Troops from Naples marched into Rome, quickly back out when a French general arrived, and saw their country turned into a new French-styled republic. But by now a livid Russia had obtained permission to march troops through Austria and the whole of

Europe was coming together in a new coalition against the French. The Directory had to respond to the possibility of a new continent-wide war with a levee en masse. But the people of France had allowed the Directory to function because it had seen an internal peace of sorts. Now the Directory seemed to be triggering the cycle of war, conscription and terror once more. The Directory's promise of stability was ruined when its own out-of-control foreign policy removed such stability. The military coups would soon involve the heads of the military, not the Directors.

For the Directory, the answer was to relaunch a great war and begin a large-scale advance against Austria, Russia and rebels everywhere. They were met by the forces of the rival great powers, and all the conquered lands fell into rebellion, including Italy.

The Wars of the Second Coalition, 1799 – 1801

The defeated First Coalition of the French Revolutionary Wars weren't defeated in their heads. While Russia, Prussia and Austria delayed any revenge plans in order to better regroup, they could see an easy path to the moral high ground and public support, not to mention public money, when France marched into the Papal Staes and Switzerland. During 1798 and early 1799 a 'Second Coalition' formed, with Britain and the Ottomans joining. This might seem odd now, but Russia was very keen to rejoin because they were livid over the French conquest of Malta—of which the Tsar considered himself protector.

However, once again there was no unified command, or even alliance, just a set of separate agreements with no overall strategy, goals or exit point. Coalition rivals would produce faultiness from the start, such as Austria's suspicions of British goals in the Netherlands, or Britain and Russia's disagreements over Malta. They even disagreed over France, with Britain wanting to end the revolution while others wanted to make some territorial gains and then agree a settlement, aka the eighteenth century model of warfare and diplomacy which the revolutionaries had torn up. Even with Napoleon absent, France could work through these cracks.

The coalition planned on advancing three armies: Russia's Suvarov was to take Austrian and Russian forces into Italy, Britain's Duke of York was to take British and Russian forces into the Netherlands, and Archduke Charles would march in the middle. However, Archduke Charles, a genuinely talented commander, found all his proposals for a central commander and a better organised attack ignored. The French, in contrast, had far fewer men (250,000 free to fight back compared to 430,000 coming) but had the Directory actually in overall charge.

Not that it mattered at first. While French forces took Naples and created a short-lived Parthenopean Republic, Jourdan's attempt to defeat Austria before Russia arrived resulted in two defeats to Archduke Charles, and Jourdan's resignation. Meanwhile, Suvarov took advantage of French problems in Italy to steamroll ahead and kill the French leader, Joubert. However, Suvarov had been ignoring instructions from above too, but the annoyed Austrians managed to get him sent to a different part of Europe, and an Austrian took over, recapturing almost everything Napoleon had done.

French's Massena replaced Jourdan and formed an Army of the Danube. Massena had been fighting in Switzerland but he could not keep Zurich. The coalition's musical chairs continued: with Suvarov on the way to help in Switzerland (having been pulled out of where he was successful), Archduke Charles was sent to the Netherlands (having been pulled out of where *he* was successful). Massena attacked and won a major victory as the coalition commanders were travelling. Suvarov arrived to repair damage and saved the army, but he had to retreat and was sacked by the Tsar.

Charles reached the Netherlands to find that front effectively finished. The British had landed, had problems, and the Duke of York had won a battle and left. Meanwhile the Tsar was having doubts. Italy had gone very well, but he was focused on failure in Switzerland and the Netherlands, believing the Austrians to be on the verge of settling, so he quit.

Then a new player emerged: Napoleon had turned into First Consul.

CRIB

- There is now a conscious effort to replace the carnage with a middle-of-the-road regime. The result is a new constitution with a five-man Directory. A final attempt by the mob fails.

- A young soldier called Napoleon comes to prominence when he and a Director tackle one of the mob's last efforts.

- The Directory balances keeping royalists (who are rising in number) and Jacobins (who want more extreme government) away from power.

- Napoleon commands the Italy's army and wins a series of stunning victories which he then turns into a political platform for his own career. France now has an embryonic empire.

- The Directory, attempting to keep royalists and Jacobins from power, stages a coup to remain in power by manipulating the election results.

- The Directory now rules through coups following elections, packing the representatives with their own handpicked members, backed by the power of the military. Political parties and democracy aren't allowed to grow.

- However, the Directory manage to get France involved in a renewed war and it goes very badly.

11: Napoleon Takes Power

Napoleon Bonaparte was stuck in the Middle East when he learned of the disasters facing the Republic. He thus decided to abandon his current army and sail secretly back to France to save the nation, and naturally to advance himself. It wasn't to be a straight coup, but it would bring about the end of the revolutionary era and open another one. How was that possible? How could all these years of chaos end? The people of France were tired and wanted stability. Not necessarily peace, but the ability to look further ahead. Yes, some wanted a king. Yes, some wanted a harder Republic. But many, many people wanted the gains of the revolution secured and a government to continue in confidence. Napoleon, as much a political genius as a military one, would bring this about by very careful conciliation and naked egotism.

In 1799 there were once more elections. This brought the lowest turnout yet as everyone knew the Directory were manipulating the results to make sure their favoured candidates appeared to be selected. The royalists boycotted, everyone else knew it was fake. There seemed no point in voting. But despite this—in fact, probably because of it—some backbone appeared, and the people the Directory thought they'd pushed into obedience provided real election results. The consequence was a council which sat in opposition to the Directory.

We now meet Sieyes again, who felt he should act. Oddly, a man who was instrumental in the start of the revolution would be instrumental in ending it. He escaped the early attacks of the newly independent Council, who unloaded on the Directors for the restarting of war, for failure in foreign policy, internal divisions and fraud. In fact, the Council was so fierce, so active, that it forced what's been called the Coup of Prairial, when three Directors were forced to quit. But this reverse coup did not secure fairness, as it had been organised by Sieyes and left Sieyes as the dominant force on the Directory.

For a time, the Jacobin faction in the Directory, which had only just been returned in significant numbers, rose in power and advanced a series of typically Jacobin laws: a new levee en masse, a tax on the noble, the ability to take hostages in threatened areas. But the Jacobins had not learned and France was not ready for extremism again. This looked so much like a move to Terror that the rest of the council expelled them.

Meanwhile, Sieyes was exploring options. He forged a link with Joubert, one of the other bright lights of the Republic's military, and the general was sent to Italy to establish himself as a true power broker ... but he was killed waging the war. History might have been different if Sieyes had staged his coup with Joubert rather than Napoleon. Yet, for a while, Council and Directory seemed to be working together. As the war was going badly, a movement to declare the 'Country in Danger' and

201

award emergency powers to the government was defeated in favour of the current system. Then the war started getting better.

But Sieyes had been waiting, and the war going well was the trigger for him to react. He wanted a strong executive, but the current constitution had been drawn up with lots of laws designed to prevent swift change. What Sieyes needed to do was take a leading military figure and use him as a figurehead in a coup which would instantly remodel the constitution, giving Sieyes much more power. Joubert, the original choice, was dead. But recently landed back in France was the dynamic and popular Bonaparte. Sieyes asked him.

Of course, Napoleon had to reach Paris first, and having landed in France on October 10th, he was acclaimed by huge crowds as he marched up to the capital, and once there everyone of any substance approached him too. Elsewhere, royalist rebels were once more causing trouble and Jacobins were fighting on too. The extremes seemed active, the war was on a knife edge, government by coup was getting tiresome. The people of France seemed ready to be aided by their undefeated hero and Napoleon knew it. Sieyes saw in Napoleon a brilliant General who could be used, and he was entirely wrong. Napoleon saw in Sieyes a cunning politician who could be used, and he was entirely right. Aided by his brother Lucien Bonaparte (who, by a stroke of luck, had become president of the Five Hundred), a plan was created. One final, great coup.

First, Lucien claimed a Jacobin plot threatened the councils and they were moved to a royal palace at Saint-Cloud, to avoid interference by the Paris mob. Napoleon was made commander of all the local soldiers. Sieyes then induced the whole Directory to resign and Napoleon appeared before the councils backed by troops and ordered a new constitution to be created to fill the void. The Five Hundred initially refused, even physically throwing Napoleon out of the chamber, but in doing so they scratched his face and Lucien stepped in, talked up the blood as a sign of attempted murder, and induced the soldiers to protect their hero and clear the council halls. They did, and enough obedient members of the Five Hundred were gathered to suspend the government and draw up a new system, and in the meantime the government would consist of three newly created 'Consuls': Sieyes, Napoleon and Ducos.

A lot of ink has been spent on why the Directory failed, but the truth is it was never allowed to work. The Directors refused to accept the results of the votes, and instead used the military to suppress both sides of France's political spectrum (royalist and Jacobin). Could the Directory in itself heal the split between these two sides? Had it been left to work and a full party-political system emerged—maybe, we cannot know, and the Directors never tried to build their own middle ground party. Certainly the royalists of 1795-9 were only working in the system to destroy it and bring a king back, while the Jacobins were the same but opposite. Napoleon didn't seize power from a working system, he ended one that just about everyone considered a pretence.

Sieyes wrote most of the new constitution. A one hundred-strong Tribunate discussed legislation which a three hundred-strong Legislative Body voted on, overseen by a Senate. A Council of State would work with Consuls. Here was the key. Sieyes wanted two Consuls created, one each for internal and external affairs, under the oversight of a ceremonial Grand Elector who had only the right to appoint the Consuls and stay in the job for life. Sieyes wanted Napoleon to be Grand Elector, but the latter refused. He wanted actual power, and got what he insisted: three Consuls, with the First Consul having deciding votes. That was to be him. If the Republic still had a Gregorian calendar, Napoleon would have had a great Christmas present, as the new constitution came into being on December 25th.

First Consul

In two years Napoleon would do much to close the wounds of the Revolution and bring the stability people wanted, while also waging war and making himself Emperor. One part of this victory was to win the war in brilliant fashion. One aspect of the French Revolutionary and Napoleonic Wars that benefitted Napoleon until near the end was the discord among the enemy coalitions, and now at this early point the First Consul benefitted from Russia falling out with the Austrians and quitting the war in 1800.

Napoleon set out to defeat Austria again, and he resolved to start with a reconquest of Italy now that other commanders had lost all his gains. He marched in May 1800, crossing the Alps via the Great Saint Bernard Pass, which the great painter and questionable revolutionary functionary David turned into a famous painting in which Napoleon rides a far larger animal than he actually used. This was a dangerous ploy but when it succeeded Napoleon found himself to the rear of his enemy and ready to cause carnage. However, this was very much the era before satellites and data, and Napoleon thought the Austrian armies were in different locations than they actually were, which was why Napoleon's force was spread out in marching order when they bumped into the entire 40,000-strong Austrian army at Marengo on June 14th. Napoleon had just 18,000 men ready to go, with the rest behind him.

The Battle of Marengo did not go brilliantly for Napoleon. An Austrian attack—utilising their larger numbers and bridges which Napoleon's reconnaissance had reported as destroyed—was looking victorious when two key things happened. The first is that Austrian commander Melas felt victory was secured, rode away from the command position and left a junior in charge. The next is French General Desaix managed to arrive at the battle with two divisions, who charged in and routed

Austria. Melas had to surrender, the army was destroyed … but Desaix, one of France's most able men and a possible rival to Napoleon's glory, had been killed, and Napoleon took sole credit. Had Napoleon lost, he might have also lost power as First Consul, but victory here, without Desaix, meant he got stronger. Elsewhere, French forces won victories which allowed them to march on Vienna, and threatened from multiple directions, Austria began peace negotiations on Christmas Day (which they still had in their calendar). The result was that the February 1801 Treaty of Lunéville. Campo Formio was confirmed, including France's absorption of Belgium and the Rhine's left bank, as well as the new Italian republics—but there was more. France turned Tuscany into a kingdom with a Bourbon king, and secured Naples under one too. Hardly the ideals of the middle revolution. Napoleon seemed to have brought peace to the continent. No one was currently at war with France except Britain, and even it temporarily gave up and signed the Peace of Amiens in early 1802. Napoleon had ended the French Revolutionary Wars on entirely positive terms for France. There now followed the only full year of peace in this entire conflict.

Napoleon had achieved a great success and could pretty much do anything he wanted now. The self-styled pretender Louis XVIII wrote and asked Napoleon to install the king onto the French throne, because that return to monarchy could alone end the divisions in France. Louis was hopelessly misjudging Napoleon, but the two were otherwise thinking along the same lines. Napoleon planned nothing less than replacing the royalist dreams and uniting the nation under himself. He started a process of conciliation. Emigres were invited back, on the condition they accepted the loss of any property, and any who had fought against France would be pardoned. Royalist rebels within France were courted. Meanwhile the Jacobins were stamped on, especially after an assassination attempt on the First Consul (which was actually by a royalist, but facts are malleable when you're trying to secure a throne).

The land issues, long a problem, were solved when Napoleon guaranteed no changes to the existing situation, bringing alongside everyone who had gained. A state bank was created to finally modernise the finances of the nation. Soldiers backed up new legal officers to bring peace inside the new borders and Napoleon personally oversaw the creation of a new, uniform set of laws in the Civil Code. Furthermore, Napoleon now came to an agreement with the Roman church.

The Concordat

The Directory had seen a Catholic revival spread across France, but there were still great tensions. Napoleon saw these, and believed he could benefit, as could France. If he could heal the religious wound which had destabilised the revolution he could secure his own position, because a damaged church undermined peace, created the friction we have seen between pious, often rural areas and anti-clerical urban centres, and could be mobilised by royalist and counter revolutionaries. A friendly church could also work to support Napoleon's position as ruler, as Catholicism was so tied to monarchy, Napoleon could tie it to his own monarchy. Napoleon had an older mindset too, believing the church could spell out to people the right way to live, which of course it always had done. However, to do this would take a bold, brave piece of diplomacy and Napoleon acted, not out of faith, but pure pragmatism.

He produced the Concordat of 1801, which was officially promulgated in 1802, a delay so Napoleon could present it after he claimed to have brought peace to maximise his power and undercut Jacobins. In the Concordat, the Pope agreed to accept the loss of church property, while France paid church officials a wage from the state, ending the separation of the two. Napoleon—well, technically the First Consul, but everyone knew who that was—had the power to nominate bishops, seminaries were made legal, the geography of parishes changed, and at the last minute Napoleon sneaked in the 'organic articles' which governed Papal control over bishops and tilted that balance in favour of the French government. Other religions were to be legal and tolerated.

The result was a few years of religious peace, with the Pope seemingly endorsing the rule of Napoleon. It went wrong, of course, when Napoleon overstretched and created an imperial catechism in 1806, which was supposed to be a series of questions and answers intended to educate / educating parishioners about Catholicism but now trained people to believe in Napoleon's own empire. Giving himself his own saint's day didn't help. This situation deteriorated to the point that the Pope excommunicated Napoleon, who used his military power to arrest the Pope, and then tried to force through the Concordat of Fontainbleau to take more power back in 1813. Yet, despite all that, the Concordat remained in place until 1905 (when the Separation Law split church and state), and Napoleon genuinely created a religious peace not seen since before the start of the revolution.

The Napoleonic Code

Napoleon also contributed something else of major importance to France (and indeed the world): The Napoleonic Code. This was actually called the Civil Code of the French People, and in 1804 was enacted everywhere France controlled, including Belgium and chunks of Italy and Germany. That other countries saw it and adopted (variations of) it further spread its power, and in 1807 it became known as the Code Napoleon. So what was it? The 'Code' was a unified set of laws which replaced the ill-fitting jigsaw that had been the French legal system. In theory, this was a code of laws written from scratch and based not on God-given power or the rule of kings (or emperors), but common sense, equality, logic and justice.

This theory fell down at various points. Women were treated as second class and subjugated to fathers and husbands, and while the idea was that all *male* citizens were equal with class now defunct, the practical effect was to dial down the liberalism of the revolutionaries. It looked to Roman law, to the security of land ownership and private property. Slavery returned, as did branding and lifelong hard labour. The Code attempted to compromise old and new and ended up favouring tradition and conservatism.

However, although the Code had been asked for during the revolution, it really did deserve to have Napoleon's name on it. Napoleon directed the teams of lawyers behind it, appearing at nearly half the Senate discussions to push things along, and he took a slow process and injected his dynamism and (not exactly liberal) ideas to get it finished.

The Napoleonic Code was divided into several 'Books'. The first concerned people—marriage, parent and child, civil rights—while the second dealt with things like property. The third focused on changes, like marriage and inheritance, while add ons followed: 1806's Code of Civil Procedure; 1807's Commercial Code; 1808's Criminal Code and Code of Criminal Procedure; 1810's Penal Code. While these Codes have been greatly modified (such as the changes to emancipate women), they essentially remain in place today.

CRIB

- A Director called Sieyes believes France needs stronger government and thinks he can use a general as a pawn. To this end he and Napoleon Bonaparte stage a coup which only just works.

- But Napoleon is a brilliant politician and a vastly successful general and he gets himself made First Consul, the most powerful man in France.

- The power of the military has replaced the mob as the violence behind the revolution.

- Napoleon now wins more victories while ending the revolution: building a consensus, gaining support from all factions, making peace with the Church and introducing laws and codes which guarantee the land redistribution but which give opportunity for royalist and Jacobin alike.

- Napoleon does this by making a new monarchy: his own dynasty. The revolution is over.

12: Napoleon: Emperor and Empire

All of this was carefully designed by Napoleon to end revolution and bring peace to France under him. The questions which had divided France were brought to a moderate end: a restored but altered church, land confirmed in its post-revolutionary state, a glorious new monarch, albeit not from the old family. A new monarch? Yes, because Napoleon wanted more permeance and power, he wanted a dynasty. He wanted it for himself. The constitution had made Napoleon First Consul, but only for ten years, and one side effect of giving security to the people was that they began to wonder what would happen when Napoleon left. Suddenly, the idea of having him remain gained traction from people who weren't just Napoleon, which was why, after semingly glowing military victory, internal peace, and a sense of compromise but strong direction, Napoleon was able to get himself named First Consul for Life in 1802 with public acclaim.

Napoleon wasn't just aided by favourable public opinion; he was still doing the old tricks of pushing his supporters into government while reducing the power of others, and by 1804 that had produced a new ruling class loyal to their First Consul. Napoleon was taking everyone who felt safer because of his ending the revolution and binding them in a web around him. But a great fear arose once more out of these new notable leaders, who were a mixture of old nobility and bourgeoisie: Napoleon led armies, so what would happen if he died doing this? Or, after an assassination attempt, if a new Corday arose? The self-styled heir to the throne still sat outside the country plotting a return, and with it the return of all 'stolen' property. England's example hung over them: a land where a civil war had ended the monarchy, only for the king to return later and execute regicides. Napoleon played on these fears to present not just himself as essential, but also the dynastic inheritance which would put an heir in power and keep the new regime going. The leaders of France called for Napoleon's position to be made hereditary.

Napoleon took this further—he wanted to be a glorious new and unifying monarch, and on May 18th, 1804 the Senate, who Napoleon had handpicked (and who, unlike the handpicked Assembly of Notables, actually did what it was told), made Napoleon Emperor of the French. King simply wasn't ambitious enough, and tied to bad memories. His family were the heirs, because Napoleon had no children, and so he could adopt a named heir or a different Bonaparte could step in. With a final bit of election fraud, a vote produced 3.5 million for, 2500 against, but cheats here had included casting an automatic yes for anyone and everyone linked to the military.

Although the Pope was at the ceremony on December 2nd, 1804 when Napoleon was made emperor, it was Napoleon who put the crown on his own head (and on the new Empress Joséphine's). Sadly, as with so many queens, Joséphine was later divorced so Napoleon could have a biological child, marrying Marie-Louise of Austria and producing Napoleon II, King of Rome. He would never rule France. Meanwhile, the Senate and Napoleon's Council of State took control and the rest of the constitution faded away.

Napoleon's Hold on France

Of course, 'ending the revolution' had a different dimension, because the revolution had been wracked and torn by the mass subscription of soldiers, yet Napoleon's wars carried on nearly continuously and would include the conscription of two million soldiers, with a vast, vast number of those dying in some foreign land. How Napoleon managed to keep control of France while waging this war has intrigued people, including those who wish to look at the twentieth century and then peer back to cast Napoleon as some sort of proto-dictator. I don't go that far, but Napoleon did use both carrots and sticks to bind France to him, replacing the chaos of the revolution with a strong, central government which involved multiple factions, as well as stamping down on opposition.

What do I mean by centralisation? A law in 1800 created the prefects. There was one of these for every department, and rather than come from representative elections they were appointed by Napoleon and worked for his central government, providing a central core and direct passage of orders through to the localities between Napoleon and taxation, propaganda, surveillance and, of course, administration. The historian Cobb called this new level of command "bureaucratic repression", while another, Godechot, called them "little emperors," which they effectively were. Yet Napoleon used this as a tool of reconciliation. His administration could afford to pay a lot of people well thanks to the looting of war, and he pulled together people who had served the various eras of the past few years, combining former enemies into a structure: old regime staff, old nobles, revolutionary deputies, directory officials, and the bourgeoisie all formed a new class of imperial notables. Fifty per cent of the prefects came from the old regime nobility into a system which welcomed them. Napoleon had solved France's factionalism and created a working central government.

That said, Napoleon did turn the rest of the government into a servile tool. The upper reaches of representative government had no major powers and were just left to support Napoleon. He packed the Senate with supporters and bought them off with honours. The members of the Tribunate were heavily reselected in 1802 after they proved too critical, and they didn't put up much opposition and were closed in 1807. Napoleon thus had a good decade of relative freedom from the representatives, until the debacle of Russia, and in 1813-14 when the Senate did finally try and reject their paymaster. However, many of these men were survivors of the revolutionary governments—only twenty-six of the first hundred tribunes were new to assemblies.

Napoleon did not want a free press, he wanted something which would promote him. To this end he attacked the press, allowing only thirteen political publications, banning new ones, heavily censoring and using the police to keep an eye on those left. Many topics were banned outright, and in 1809 Napoleon gave every paper their own dedicated censor. All books, plays and even posters had to be submitted for approval. By 1810-11, the clampdown left each department with just one newspaper (Paris could have four). It was actually worse than that, because Napoleon loved wandering around dictating letters and documents, and he wrote a large proportion of the articles which filled *Le Moniteur*, the government paper. Dissent could not easily be shared.

Speaking of the police... Napoleon wanted the legal system tied to him, so he ended the election of judges and appointed them all, allowing him to create a whole tier who owed him, and which he could keep a close eye on. In addition a new system of 'judicial tribunals' was installed. But this wasn't just arresting thieves—far from it. The Ministry of General Police was a massive surveillance organisation looking into enemies of the state, managing food prices and tracking down the considerable number of deserters from the armies. We now come to the bit that most reminds people of dictatorship: Napoleon was given daily intelligence reports on the state of the nation, and dissenters all had files kept. To be fair, the Terror had imprisoned and executed thousands of people for no good reason at all, and Napoleon tended to favour house arrest over the guillotine. There was also a turn to the surreal: there were spies spying on the spies.

Napoleon was lucky. He knew he was lucky, and one way was in agriculture. The years before the revolution had seen awful weather and harvests, which was a major problem in a nation where most of the economy functioned around agriculture, and where most of the nation were still peasants. But Napoleon had tremendous luck in that most of the harvests during his era were good ones, which kept prices affordable, reducing the likelihood of rural and urban rebellion. There were two exceptions: 1802-3, though Napoleon was riding high on (temporary) peace, and in 1811-12, when a bad harvest caused disturbances which turned into major unrest when news of the Russian disaster spread.

Russia was, however, later in Napoleon's career, and for most of his time in charge he was successful, by which I mean he won victory after victory. And here's the crucial point: he won them abroad. The conflict was kept off French soil, bringing in loot and giving the people spared from the armies the delusion that everything was okay. Military victory created a sense of

217

glory for France and the supporters of Napoleon, and many people bought it. The vast quantities of stolen wealth gained by the victories helped the regime run smoothly. Only when these victories dried up did the shine leave the glory, did taxes and internally produced military spending have to rise, as the reputation of their ruler was broken. It's worth noting that Napoleon solved a major revolutionary tension between the heads of the government and the heads of the military by combining them into one person, himself, which did cut short a lot of previous arguments.

The money was important, because Napoleon could gain allies and keep them through a mixture of bribery and patronage which had no dividing line down the middle. Napoleon effectively created a vast body of supporters, indeed a new imperial aristocracy, by paying them. Land, titles, money, positions of power, all were handed out, as were new awards like the Legion of Honour (mostly given to the military), and 3,600 titles of which a fifth were the old nobles and four fifths the military. Hereditary titles even returned, but Napoleon's cunning was to give large grants of land to people and make these grants outside France in an attempt to invest the new notables in keeping the Napoleon empire in existence. Napoleon took the warring faction of the revolution and bound them to him. For instance, at one point his co-consuls were Lebrun, a royalist administrator, and Cambacérès, an ex-noble

218

and Jacobin. In this way the Napoleonic system unified a fractured France, and did so as long as he was winning. Indeed, the whole regime was founded on military success with military men in charge. What this meant was that upward mobility ceased for those at the bottom of society. Economics underpinned it: the leading taxpayers across France were landowners, professionals, merchants, and Napoleon studied them, buttressed their landholdings with the Code and the Concordat, gave them and their heirs roles in the government. Equally, while the chance to rise was reduced, the peasants of France had benefitted in a small way from land redistribution and in a large way from Napoleon confirming these changes.

Having said Napoleon censored other people's creativity, we need to stress he was a huge lover of culture as a way of promoting himself, and sponsored masses of art in an attempt to bolster his own image and swamp opposition. Great paintings and sculptures were produced from his patronage

The Napoleonic Regime was created and maintained by a range of tactics, but ultimately it needed Napoleon to keep winning to stay together. He didn't manage to create something that would last in peace, partly because a combination of the state of Europe and his own slightly manic drive meant there wasn't peace for it to grow into, and once Napoleon began to lose after 1912, the system fell apart. When the sixth coalition armies marched into Paris to reject Napoleon, there was no

219

crazed massacres or defence. Yet, in a strange way, despite the wars Napoleon brought considerable stability after what had come before.

Aside: Napoleon's Empire

The borders of France blurred during the revolution, and changed even more during the Napoleonic Wars as France gained greater and greater control of foreign places. On May 12th, 1802, this group became an official Empire, with the hereditary Emperor Bonaparte. By 1810 it's easier to list the parts of Europe that Napoleon wasn't dominating: Portugal, Sicily, Sardinia, Montenegro, and the British, Russian and Ottoman empires. Yet the Napoleonic Empire wasn't a monolithic structure, and while the french revolutionaries had pushed their 'freedom' onto other states, the result of all these wars was a jigsaw of friction like the old regime before.

The empire was actually a three-tier system. The Pays Réunis comprised / designated all the areas ruled by the classic French administration in Paris. This included all of France inside the natural frontiers (the Alps, the Rhine and the Pyrenees), and Holland, Piedmont, Parma, the Papal States, Tuscany, the Illyrian Provinces and more of Italy. Each of these was divided into departments, and in 1811, the height f of empire, totalled 130 departments with forty-four million people. Then there was the Pays Conquis, which actually is what it sounds: the conquered, although theoretically independent, countries ruled by people Napoleon approved of and often appointed, which basically meant his family or his loyal commanders. Technically, they were a buffer from attack, but in practice they were states given as presents, and as the wars progressed they expanded and shrank. They included the Confederation of the Rhine, Spain, Naples, the Duchy of Warsaw and parts of Italy. Finally there were the Pays Alliés, which were countries who had managed to retain independence, but which had been beaten at times and often had to listen to what Napoleon had to say. They included Napoleon's enemies, namely Prussia, Austria and Russia. They were not happy 'allies'. A new word emerged: the Grand Empire, formed from the Pays Réunis and Pays Conquis, and in 1811, it included 80 million people. To create this, Napoleon redrew the middle of Europe, erasing another empire: the Holy Roman Empire ended on August 6th, 1806, the end of a thousand years.

Nature of the Empire

The empire had great regional variation, partly depending on how long each region stayed part of it (changes could become embedded or quickly rejected when other armies marched in), and this depended on whether they were in the Pays Réunis or Pays Conquis. Some historians say time wasn't actually relevant to this, and the nature of the Napoleonic state was dependant on the nature of the areas before he arrived, with local, long-term variations affecting what Napoleon could do in each. As you've seen above, the Pays Réunis departmentalized. The changes of the revolution were carried into this, so 'feudalism' was cancelled and land redistributed. Both Pays Réunis and Pays Conquis saw the implementation of the Concordat, the Napoleonic legal Code and, of course (and primarily), tax demands.

Napoleon also innovated, and by that I mean he developed looting. He created 'dotations', which was conquered land from which the entire revenue was officially assigned to Napoleon's favourites as a reward: if you stayed loyal and worked to maintain the empire, this benefit lasted for you and your heirs. They were a huge loss to local economies, such as in the Duchy of Warsaw, which lost 20% of its annual revenue to dotations. Napoleon wasn't spreading the Code and the end of the old regime out of ideology or love for the revolution. He was doing it for pragmatic survival, and accepted far more old regime practices than the revolution ever had.

This empire didn't last for very long, but we can clearly see attempts—and successes—to centralise these states to a larger extent as he put into practice a full European empire. If there had been more Napoleons, or he'd been in more places at once, this transformation would have been quicker, but it was greatly

222

affected by the quality of the subordinates Napoleon put in charge. Some were deeply able and interested in their new land rather than aiding their patron and didn't do what he wanted, while some were poorly skilled for land management and failed to carry out his wishes. Most of the Bonaparte men proved to be poor local rulers. Beauharnais installed a stable government in Italy which proved very popular, but Napoleon prevented him from going further. Brother Louis in Holland rejected most of what Napoleon wanted to happen and was thrown out by him. Of course, Spain under the barely competent brother Joseph couldn't really have been more of a disaster.

Officially, Napoleon promoted his empire as defending the revolution against the counter-revolutionary forces of empire coupled with a desire to free all the oppressed. In practice, he wasn't driven by any of that. He almost certainly didn't start his career wanting to rule all of Europe in a universal monarchy, but as his success grew his ego and ambition expanded to match. Napoleon's vista was ever expanding, and it was driven by personal hunger for power and wealth. It was also driven by the need to feed the system he had created. France had been bound around Napoleon by glory and reward, so Napoleon had to create thrones and crowns and find land to give to his family and followers. This form of patronage had worked for centuries, but it always came with the same need to find increasing rewards, so he had to keep fighting and expanding, and that cost huge sums of money to supply greater armies than had been used before. The empire became the source of funds and troops: food, money, equipment, soldiers themselves, all were pulled out of the empire.

This empire was never given time to bed in. It could only survive as long as the military victories which created it were sustained. Napoleon's many faulty appointments could be masked, but only by soldiers and glory. Once Napoleon failed, the empire dissolved as it had not lasted long enough to become its own structure without him. A common source of debate is if Napoleon had lasted, would the empire have survived and formed a unified (of sorts) Europe, or was this simply a continental colonialism that would have eaten itself and failed? That all said, a lot of the structures Napoleon put it place survived long after him: the more bureaucratic states, opportunities for the bourgeoisie, the codes, religious toleration and secular control in church land and roles. The Napoleonic Empire lasted in a way, just without Napoleon.

13: Conclusions

Aftermath: The Restoration

In 1813 to 14, France's enemies actually united in a complete coalition, exploited the fact Napoleon could not be in more than one place at a time, took advantage of the damage he'd done to his army and reputation in Russia, and forced the emperor to abdicate. However, the victorious allies of Europe needed someone to rule France instead. But who? Napoleon, and some other powers, wanted his son to become Napoleon II. After all, the boy's mother was an Austrian princess of the highest order. But Britain led the party who wanted all the Bonapartes gone, and that included Napoleon II. Some looked to Bernadotte, a former commander in Napoleon's army who had turned against his old leader but managed to still get himself made King of Sweden. On this occasion he was deemed too Napoleonic. The other obvious solution was to bring someone from the royal family, the Bourbons, back, and restore the French monarchy. No thought was given to restoring the republic, which the other heads of Europe associated with the destruction of their own power.

Which Monarch?

The deposed king had been executed, and his son had died during the years of Napoleon. The allies would have to widen the search for the restoration, which gave them two branches of the royal family. On the one hand, they had the brother of the old king, who already called himself Louis XVIII, and already thought he was king of France. The allies knew he would have problems making himself popular with a French populous radically, perhaps permanently, changed by the revolution. He was 59, looked like a physical embodiment of royal excess, had spent much of his life outside France plotting against the leaders within and would be arriving thanks to enemy bayonets.

There was another choice, a younger and more distant member, Louis-Philippe, duc d'Orléans, whose father had been a supporter of the revolution in the initial period and seemed likely to work with the existing French state to build a consensus. The allies had the not inconsiderable problem of how to ignore Louis XVIII for Louis-Philippe given that the former had the stronger claim. The allies disagreed over it, and then decided to cover their disagreement by pretending they were letting 'the French' decide. Luckily for Louis XVIII, one of the era's great survivors was in position to help him: Talleyrand was back, the diplomat who had moved through the revolution and survived a break with Napoleon to campaign against him, wanted Louis XVIII, and was able to turn the Paris press, now already disposed to the royalist cause, to create the impression it was what the people wanted. Then one of those oddities of history occurred: Wellington's army advanced into a spontaneous display of loyalty to Louis in Bordeaux, and the allies decided the French wanted Louis XVIII.

There were problems. There was little mass opposition to the Napoleonic regime in France, as Napoleon had been careful to bring as many people into his orbit as possible, with the result that the country had an ingrained loyalty to the once Emperor and weren't spontaneously keen on anyone replacing him. The new ruler was being parachuted in, with support from rebels and exiles. The monarchy would never escape that fact and criticism.

Louis, Napoleon, Louis

To the surprise of many, Louis XVIII offered to concede to some of the changes that had happened during the revolution if he could then become king. If it was acknowledged that he was a God-given ruler on Earth with no limit on his power he'd self-impose a few limits on himself because he was magnanimous. With this unusual situation accepted, the Charter of 1814 was written by a combination of Louis' people and old Napoleonic administrators who knew what condition France was in, to create a new ruling framework. It was published on June 4th, 1814 and had 74 articles. The result was a French monarchy that not only accepted many of the revolution's changes, but which

227

was now one of the most liberal nations in Europe. However, although it was a constitutional monarchy drawing on Britain for inspiration, it was not a parliamentary democracy, and the king had great power: he could choose who he wanted as ministers, had a veto on all amendments to the laws only he could suggest, could name who he wanted to run the army. Point 14 gave the monarch massive emergency powers, although Louis decided not to use them.

For a while, the tiny fraction of the French nation who could vote (they had wealth, usually land) waited to see what would happen. Only around 100,000 people paid enough tax to vote, and only 15,000 qualified for election. Many of the structures of the empire were retained, such as much of the tax system, the regional officials, the bureaucracy, and most of the people who had worked in them. Even the politicians stayed mostly the same. The exiles who had dreamed of a return to France found themselves frustrated in not being better reintroduced by the king.

The war was over, the surviving soldiers returned, Louis reined himself in. Might it work? He made a few mistakes which raised eyebrows, like changing the flags back, but he made a major one when he refused to pay Napoleon's pension, leaving the former emperor close, annoyed, and nearly broke. Napoleon sailed to France, found the army flocking to him (Louis had mishandled their financial arrangements too), and

Louis fled once more. Napoleon knew he had to win victories and divide the allies so they would split and accept him, but defeat at Waterloo led to another abdication and exile to St. Helena.

Louis XVIII came back, but found a different France. The allies had been generous in 1814, but the support Napoleon received caused the allies to change their minds. France faced paying for the war, being reduced to pre-revolutionary borders, and a million troops were stationed inside to force the point home. Louis was associated with the punishment, with being against Napoleon, and even now some knew his regime would struggle. Yet he inherited a country whose infrastructure and economy had mostly survived intact. Louis ruled until his death in 1824 and kept his position as king.

Conclusions

The French Revolution had utterly changed France. Sometimes you'll see people theorise what would have happened to France without these changes and how it might have developed anyway, but that's not really relevant because the French Revolution was what happened, and that's what has to be dealt with. The people in France were left as citizens, not subjects, of their government. Even though France was beaten by the armies of Europe, the new king they produced could not resurrect the old regime. Monarchy had changed. Now voting was the key event in political life, not royal appointment, and the centralised government was built on more equal foundations. A political culture had been developed which simply would not, would never, go away.

That said, some benefitted and some suffered. Approximately one percent of France died in the revolution, and the wars would kill a million; 8.5% of French land changed ownership, and half of the nobility lost chunks. But a sixth of the families in France bought this land, and the nobility might have been reduced, but were still the majority of landowners. Indeed, less than ten per cent of nobles fled, and generally speaking those who were gaining wealth before the revolution were those who gained from it. The poor were no better off materially, and the economy was stalled for decades. Yet people had proven groups could get together and change the world they lived in. Not always for the better; in fact sometimes human nature unleashed horrors. But change they could.

The Guillotine

This narrative has mostly avoided the gory descriptions some accounts love to go into, so it might seem strange we've all arrived at a chapter about the guillotine. However, given that this is one of the most famous symbols of the revolution, and given that there's still some misconceptions about it, I'm going to explore it here.

Devices which beheaded people had existed long before the guillotine was even dreamed of, and one of the earliest was the Halifax Gibbet in Britain. Executioners with swords and axes were, however, much more common. The thing was that execution methods weren't pragmatic ways to dispatch people, they were part of public ceremonies tied into justice, punishment and conformity. France, as you've probably gathered from this book, had huge regional variation, but they had many brutal methods of bloody and agonising deaths to make a spectacle and send a warning about what was happening. People could be tied to a wheel and smashed into pieces with axes, burned alive and many other things. But if you were rich and powerful you could avoid all this and demand to be beheaded with a blade. More privilege based on social status, and a populace who were used to horrible violence, the sort of population who could then massacre people in prisons and march around with their heads on pikes. France, thanks to the public tortures, was able to carry out this brutality.

There was plenty of opposition to all this, thanks mainly to Enlightenment philosophy, where titans like Voltaire and Locke demanded something humane instead. On the second day of the debate drawing up a new penal code for the newly 'freed' France (October 10th, 1789), Dr Joseph-Ignace Guillotin proposed six articles on the reforms. Five often get ignored, and they include setting a national standard for punishment, removing variation; not seizing the property of the deceased; corpses were to be returned to the family, and those families were not to be discredited by the actions of their relative. There was the sixth point: Guillotin called for all executions in France to be carried out by decapitation, which was to be done by a machine with no torture. To this end, Guillotin attached a picture of such a creation, which was a highly ornate stone column with a falling blade in the centre, and a thin executioner leading proceedings which were hidden from the public eye, because Guillotin wanted to dignify the public and the victim. It's unclear if Guillotin's end game was to abolish the death penalty completely, but either way, some accounts describe the doctor being laughed out of the chamber. Yet Guillotin proposed the laws again on December 1st, 1789 and had the first five accepted; the machine was again, rejected.

The Assembly discussed a great many issues over the next few months, and even pondered scrapping the death penalty outright. It was in 1791 when they agreed to keep executions, and the deputies started a search for a more egalitarian way of dispatching people because the old regime was seen as brutal and horrific. The Assembly duly accepted a proposal for beheading to be the only option, but this didn't come from Guillotin, it actually came from a repetitive proposal by the Marquis Lepeletier de Saint-Fargeau. "Every person condemned to the death penalty shall have his head severed." Guillotin didn't exactly rush up to approve this: he'd given up on the plan, and might have thought he'd be remembered by history as the man who led the deputies to the tennis court where they took their oath. But the hunt was on for a method, because swords and axes had some great problems: executioners needed to be skilled or things became agonising and messy, and executioners were people and tired. France's chief executioner, Charles-Henri Sanson, championed a machine which would allow the executioners to work efficiently.

The Assembly liked the idea, and they used their general prosecutor, Pierre-Louis Roederer, to get advice from the Secretary of the Academy of Surgery in France: Doctor Antoine Louis. He designed a machine which was to be quick and painless, and the design was passed to a German engineer called

Tobias Schmidt. We don't know if Louis knew about any earlier machines, but he produced one and Schmidt built a test guillotine and tried it: first on animals, then on human bodies. What he and Louis had come up with was two fourteen-foot uprights with a crossbar, whose insides were grooved and greased to allow a weighted blade to slide down at speed. A rope and pulley operated, and the whole thing was on a high platform for public enjoyment. Final testing took place on specially chosen bulky bodies, before the first execution of a living man occurred on April 25th, 1792 when the highwayman Nicholas-Jacques Pelletier was executed. Roederer looked at a report on use and introduced the angled blade. The Assembly accepted the design, and sent copies to the provinces.

What's unusual is that at this point the machine was known as the 'Louisette' or 'Louison', after Dr Louis. Then this name vanished and a new batch of nicknames emerged before, Dr Guillotin's name resurfaced, and the machine became linked with him. We don't know when it changed from Guillotin to Guillotine, but the reason might have been to rhyme the name in song. Dr Guillotine hated this.

The design went out, to be operated in identical manner, wiping away the regional variations of old regime France, a perfect, but horrible, reflection of the revolution's ideals. The guillotine was designed to administer a fast and painless death to anyone, regardless of age, sex or wealth, a bizarre attempt to embody such concepts as equality and humanity. Timing now kicked in, as only months later the Terror was introduced, and the guillotine became synonymous with the mass executions even though its speed was too slow for the numbers and people had to be shot en masse.

The guillotine was burned into public imagination / memory by the Terror, turning into a cultural symbol. When the Terror reduced, even children's toys used its image, and 'Victims' Balls' became fashionable where the relatives of the executed attended with their hair done up and their necks exposed to reflect the doomed. Nicknames like 'the national razor', 'the widow', and 'Madame Guillotine' developed, and the guillotine doesn't seem to have been hated, or the people behind it. Extremists even praised Saint Guillotine, who'd saved them from despotism.

France used the guillotine for a long time. Only in 1939 did public executions end, nearly one hundred and fifty years after Guillotine originally asked the practice to be hidden, and the death penalty was only abolished in 1981, taking the Guillotine with it.

Dr Guillotin died of natural causes in 1814. He never made peace with the name.

Marie-Antoinette

Marie Antoinette was the eleventh daughter of the Empress Marie Theresa and Emperor Francis I, born in 1755. She was named Marie, exactly like all her other sisters, as a show of devotion to the Virgin Mary, so to differentiate between them all she was also known as Antonia, which years later would become Antoinette in France. Marie has frequently been accused of being unintelligent, whereas in fact she proved able at what she was taught, it's just that she had a bad tutor and wasn't taught much of worth, which was a bit strange given how powerful her mother was. Either way, Marie was an imperial daughter in a world full of international diplomacy, so she was actually a pawn in a much larger game. In 1756, long-term enemies France and Austria signed a peace deal to oppose Prussia, and in 1770 a marriage alliance was made between the two countries because that was basically the one way royals sealed deals. Marie Antoinette was married to the heir to the French throne, Dauphin Louis. She had to be quickly taught French.

This was how a teenage Marie found herself in a foreign country that hated her. Hated her? The French hadn't overcome their years of antipathy towards Austria, and weren't keen on this interloper. She was also now in the court of Versailles, a carefully constructed and entirely fake world governed by fiercely protected rule of etiquette which Marie openly thought stupid. But she tried to adopt the customs, and took on the role of a humanitarian.

Princesses (and queens) were expected to walk about looking regal and produce heirs. This was a world in which any lack of royal heirs would be blamed on the woman, even when the reason Marie's marriage was unconsummated for so long, and then so sexless, was probably a fault with Louis, most likely a mental one. Before you think the French were being unfair, Marie's mother blamed her too. Already, Marie was the target of gossip, and Marie collected around her a tiny circle of loyal and genuine court friends, whom the gossip mongers of the time accused her of sleeping with, both men and women.

Louis became Louis XVI in 1774, and as we've seen his actions with the parlements left him initially very popular. Even Marie was too. Now, the queen had little interest in court intrigue, of which there was a lot, and the nature of her small group of favourites upset the rest of court because Marie was drawn to lonely foreigners just like her. However, she was meant to be interested in court because Marie Theresa, and then the next Austrian emperor, constantly ordered Marie to dominate Louis and direct French affairs. She didn't.

Marie coped with her loneliness and uncertainty by trying to distract herself, but as she did it in dancing, shopping, gambling and all the other ways a queen was allowed to act she was accused of frivolity, even though she was acting out of fear and doubt. As such Marie ran an expensive court, but then again she was supposed to. However, as the French crown now wandered into a financial crisis Marie came into focus as the free spending, airheaded woman who was ruining the country. Her spending, her foreign friends, her lack of an heir... Marie was attacked by violent pornography and vicious slander. She responded by actively trying to reshape the monarchy into a new fashion. She rejected stern formality, preferring friendly, personal touches. Old fashions were rejected, and simpler, pastoral styles came in. Marie disliked the ceremony and weight of Versailles and preferred smaller, simpler worlds, and Louis agreed. Once again, the public of France reacted by attacking her, for literally anything.

In 1778 Louis had finally managed to perform and Marie gave birth to a girl, while the much-desired male heir followed in 1781. Marie moved away from public court to be with this new family, but she was soon accused by the press of having cheated, and people wondered who the fathers of these children were. Marie could no longer ignore the rumours. She was accused of being debauched, ignorant, wasteful and running France (although ironically she'd been sent to run France and wasn't). The Diamond Necklace Affair further ruined her reputation, through absolutely no fault of her own, and she took the blame.

Marie now listened to the call of her family and involved herself in the politics of France, including going to government meetings. At this time, the finances of the kingdom were ruined, and France fell into revolution, first when the king tried to force reform through an Assembly of Notables. As this situation spiralled out of control Louis became depressed, and Marie faced both a sick husband and a long-term sick son, falling into depression herself too. Yet she started to push decisions, and was responsible for the recall of Necker to the government, which was widely praised, although when her eldest son died shortly after, she grew more depressed. Marie was openly despised by the crowds of France, and her friends were fleeing the country. She stayed out of duty to her family and her husband, who refused to flee. That said, she did try to persuade her husband to flee Paris and Versailles and go to a loyal army. This was rejected, and while it would have started a civil war, it might also have saved all their lives. When a mob broke into Versailles to abuse the king, Marie just escaped a sub-mob who'd sought to kill her, and the royal family were taken to Paris as prisoners. Falling deeper into depression, Marie deliberately hid herself away so as to avoid antagonising the mob.

Marie lived in a strange half-world for a while, taking on the main role of negotiating in secret with Mirabeau and finally judging him unhelpful, and arranging for the family to flee to

239

France, but they had left it too late and only got to Varennes before being caught. Marie then negotiated with deputies on the manner of the constitutional monarchy, all in a semi-secret state. When France and Austria entered into a war, Marie became an enemy of the state, a literal one as she gave whatever information she could to her birth family in Austria to aid their advance. But the royals were overthrown, arrested, Marie's closest friend was murdered and her head shown on a pike to the royal prison, and then Louis was executed.

Now known as Widow Capet, Marie was the subject of a power struggle in the French government between those who wanted to exchange her with Austria or try and execute her. Also known as Prisoner No. 280, she could not see her son. Finally Marie was tried in a fake court. Here she had to listen to abuse after abuse, lie after lie, including the claim that she molested her son, before the only even remotely likely verdict was read out: guilty. She was executed on October 16th, 1793.

Robespierre

Robespierre was born into a lawyers' family in Arras, France. His mother died when he was six, and his often-absent father seemed to care little before he vanished for good. Robespierre's sister later said that this experience produced a serious and solitary character in her brother; it's possible this gave Robespierre the empathy with those rejected by society that he seemed to possess when older. Even at a young age Robespierre had little tolerance for failure and an ability to hold grudges; he was also, as always, thin and pale.

He won a scholarship to study in Paris, where on one occasion he was chosen to give a speech to King Louis XVI. He performed well in law and philosophy, graduating with a law degree and a prize for his ability in 1781. By now he had read, and was deeply affected by, Rousseau. Nevertheless, Robespierre remained cautious, reserved and something of a dreamer. He returned to Arras where he practised law and soon became a judge and chancellor of the Arras Academy, while earning a reputation as someone who represented the poor and oppressed. His writings won him both a competition and the fear of the rich.

Early Days of the Revolution: Rise to Prominence

When the Estates General was summoned in 1788, Robespierre was very keen to be involved and produced a text demanding reform, partly so he would be able to gain election, and partly to attack what we might consider abuses of power. He was elected to represent the region; he was thirty. Robespierre had a weak voice, was only a moderate speaker and never lost his nerves entirely; he was also a minor figure on the national stage. But he carefully studied the techniques used by the popular deputies to win support. Growing in confidence, and taking advantage of his position as a radical who could demand attention, he soon earned himself a reputation from his speeches in the National Assembly and was accorded the benefit of suffering opposition attacks: he became part of the conversation, a piece of public opinion.

From 1789 to 1792 he made over a hundred speeches which transformed him into the leader of the left, and the leader of democratic ideals aimed as enfranchising the poor. Although Robespierre was overlooked for high office in the government of the time—he coveted the role of leader of the revolution and took advantage of his opportunities to further himself—he focused greatly on pushing France into reform and argued for universal suffrage, an end to the death penalty and the opening up of the military's officer class. He also tried people in court based on their character, not on their crimes. He also became the de facto leader of the Jacobins.

Leading the Jacobins

As the new constitutional monarchy was being planned and created, Robespierre planned for life as Public Prosecutor of Paris, being illegible to stand for election of the new National Assembly through his own laws. However, after King Louis XVI had tried to flee France, Robespierre held the Jacobins together after many less extreme members left, and after the creation of the new Assembly he still spoke frequently in the Jacobin club. At the same time he was constantly verbally attacked over the extent of the reforms he wanted. He opposed those who wanted to use the French army to spread the revolution abroad, worrying more about counter-revolutionaries inside France, and when the French declarations of war heralded invasion, many flocked to Robespierre. He became known as the Incorruptible, for never taking bribes, for his impeccable purity, for never seeming to be wrong. He began to believe his own propaganda.

Although he was cautious about the armed rebellion which followed in August 1792, despite having written in favour of an insurrection, he was soon nominated to the Insurrectionary Commune of Paris and attempted to direct the mob to his political enemies during the September Massacres. Robespierre established the Revolutionary Tribunal to try counter-revolutionary suspects quicker, and by this time was perfectly

243

willing to sanction violence in order to advance or secure the revolution, and said so in his speeches. He was then elected to the new National Convention by Parisians. Robespierre called for the execution of the king and the redirection of the Revolutionary Wars. When others called for a dictator many believed they meant Robespierre. Meanwhile, many of Robespierre's friendships had deteriorated as he grew suspicious. He did make one new, passionate bond, with a young revolutionary called Saint-Just, who had similar views on virtue.

Insurrection, the Committee of Public Safety and the Terror

The king was, after a fierce debate, executed. With some parts of France now in open rebellion and the war looking just as dangerous, a Committee of Public Safety was created in 1793 to run the country and crush counter revolution. Robespierre spoke more and more / increasingly about secret plots and hidden enemies, and envisaged a strong central government with no split between legislative and executive. Again he was accused of wanting to be a dictator. Robespierre also frequently spoke about dying as a martyr, and attacked enemies who he thought wanted to take the benefits of the revolution away from the poor. As Robespierre and the Jacobins worked to outflank the Girondins, he grew exhausted, but he was successful.

Becoming increasingly more pragmatic—able to suspend rights to meet needs—he focused solely on the revolution.

As the overall situation worsened, Robespierre joined the Committee and moved against enemies who included former close friends, to continue the Terror and secure the revolution. The Herbertistes, Danton and friends: all went to the guillotine. With support from people he'd appointed to positions of power, holding multiple positions himself in an increasingly centralized government, the Paris commune, the mob and the Jacobins, Robespierre now basically became the government. Not a dictator, but the most powerful man in France. Now he never shied from enforcing the Terror brutally.

During 1794, Robespierre began to fully crystallise his ideas of how the new French republic should be run. He developed a desire to 'cleanse' France and create a Republic of Virtue, a utopia, and this purity was to be achieved by guillotining anyone who offended Robespierre's new moral guidelines. Robespierre himself was an exemplar, having never been caught up with bribes, sexual peccadilloes or ever admitting a mistake. Executions, which had begun to fall in numbers, now rose again. Power was increasingly concentrated in the hands of just Robespierre, and he worked to break the power of the Paris mob. Robespierre opposed atheism strongly and introduced a new religion, the Cult of the Supreme Being, also proposing free education for all children.

245

Decline and Execution: Thermidor

As Robespierre's reforms spread, so did opposition to him. The strain of running France and constantly speaking in public frequently affected his health—he had suffered from illness at times of great political decision—and he became more aloof and separate from the rest of the government, restricting his speeches to just the Jacobin club. He quickly lost many of his supporters, who were afraid he was both turning into a dictator and threatening their own safety.

A tired, paranoid Robespierre returned to the Convention to try and shore up his position, but gave a speech which attacked just about everyone, prompting his enemies to act and use the Convention to arrest him. The Paris Commune gathered to save Robespierre, but he had taken steps to break its power and it was forced to disperse. Robespierre shot himself but somehow only ended up with severe with injuries to his jaw, and was executed on July 28th, 1794; eighty supporters followed him to the blade over the next twenty-four hours. Changes in government and a devolution of power swiftly followed.

Robespierre and the Revolution

Robespierre has been identified with the revolution more than anyone else. For many, he *is* the revolution, and Robespierre almost certainly thought of himself in this way too. Of course, these people are divided over whether he represents the cold, ideology-driven bloodthirstiness of revolution, or if he was a pragmatic defender of liberty and social democracy. Examining Robespierre's life, without the bitter hindsight of rivals who saw every phase of Robespierre's youth as the path to a jealous, inhuman monster, has led some to question whether he actually went insane. What is certain is that he was always acting sincerely in trying to establish his republic of virtue, but also inhumanely, and with a total inability to compromise. What Robespierre actually meant by this republic has never been entirely explained, not by Robespierre or later writers. His recent biographer, Ruth Scurr, sums it up thus:

> "...a democracy for the people, who are intrinsically good and pure of heart; a democracy in which poverty is honourable, power innocuous, and the vulnerable safe from oppression; a democracy that worships nature – not nature as it really is, cruel and disgusting, but nature sanitised, majestic and above all good."
> (Scurr, Fatal Purity, p. 324.)

But in order to achieve this republic, Robespierre made a pact with violence, and spiralled ever further into ruthless bloodshed because for him the end always justified the means. It is this which affects his legacy more than his utopianism ever will.

Napoleon: Before and After

Napoleon wasn't just the 'Corsican Ogre', but a man of fascinating contradictions. He was a great military commander who exceeded the limits of technology to organise world-changing armies, but was also a risk-taking gambler with great impatience. He was a workaholic, a vicious cynic who could order thousands to their deaths but could and did forgive his closest betrayers; a man who could enthral other men. He would rise from very little at the perfect time and come to dominate post-revolutionary France because he was the one person who made the period post-revolutionary.

Corsica

Given that Napoleon became emperor of a French-led empire, it sometimes surprises people to know he was born in Ajaccio on Corsica, on August 15th, 1769. His father was Carlo Buonaparte (not a spelling error), a lawyer with both eyes on climbing the political ladder. His mother was Marie-Letizia. The Buonapartes were members of the Corsican nobility, which wasn't very high on the ladder compared to mainland French nobility, so they had minor wealth and were considered pretentious. Carlo was an expert social climber, Letizia had a very beneficial affair with the Comte de Marbeuf, aka the French military governor, and this got him into the military academy at Brienne in 1779. He was a talented pupil and progressed to the Parisian École Royale Militaire in 1784 and graduated a year later as a second lieutenant in the artillery. It has to be said the artillery was not the glamorous part of the military, but following his father's death in 1785, Napoleon had done a three-year course in just one.

Corsican Mistakes

In theory, Napoleon was posted on the French mainland. In practice, he spent a large amount of the next eight years in Corsica interfering in politics because of a very spirited campaign of letter writing, excuse making and rule bending, followed by some judicious avoiding of the various stages of the French revolution. However, Napoleon didn't get everything right in his life and he got Corsica completely wrong. At first he supported a local rebel and patron of his father, Pasquale Paoli. Initial success and promotion in the mainland army was scuppered when Napoleon fell out with Paoli and Corsica collapsed into the civil wars affecting France. Napoleon and his family had to flee to France, where they adopted the French version of their name (Bonaparte) and started again.

Rises and Falls

Napoleon didn't experience a straight-up rise to power. While the revolution had shattered the officer class, allowing people to experience rapid rises, they could also go back down the same well and Napoleon's fortunes changed along with his patrons. In December 1793 he was a hero after success at Toulon, a general and looked on favourably by Robespierre, but when the latter fell Napoleon was arrested for treason. Napoleon had always shown a great flexibility when it came to changing affairs, and he managed to gain the patronage of Barras as he became a Director. Heroic status returned in 1795 when Napoleon aided Barras by using troops and cannon to repel an angry mob, and the reward was rapid promotion to the upper echelons of French military society. Here, Napoleon opined on anything and everything, building himself up in public opinion. He married Joséphine de Beauharnais.

Napoleon and the Army of Italy

In 1796, Napoleon gained the post he had campaigned for: command of the Army of Italy. This wasn't an obvious outlet for glory, given it was supposed to be a distraction force, but using verve, clever words, cunning tactics and an awful lot of cold, hard cash, he turned he inexperienced, poorly supplied and very annoyed Army of Italy into a crack force which won victory after victory. Not only did Napoleon advance the cause of France, but himself too, as he dictated a peace which established him as a major and semi-independent political player on the European map. He would turn himself into an Emperor.

The Fall of the Emperor

After becoming Emperor, the wars did not stop. A restless man who believed his status depended on constant glory, Napoleon pushed his troops ever further. Spain became an open wound he could never bandage or barely even attend to, and his army became worn down. Yet he continued to keep the potential coalitions divided until the growing opposition of Russia led Napoleon on one of history's great misadventures. Gathering an army beyond the technical capabilities of the age, in 1812 Napoleon marched into Russia but found he could not bring them to surrender, and the army was destroyed by the winter. Although Napoleon performed miracles in reconstituting the French forces and fought on, the coalition finally came to full potential and exploited the fact the French emperor couldn't be everywhere at once. Enemy armies once more reached French soil, and with collapsing support in Paris—including that of his own family—Napoleon abdicated in defeat.

The coalition did not guillotine Napoleon—this was not the revolutionaries of France acting. Instead they exiled him to Elba. But Bonaparte grew bored and found a way to return to the mainland, where the new king fled and soldiers flocked to a reborn emperor. Had he learned from his mistakes? Maybe not. The plan was to gather an army and win a brilliant victory which would divide the coalition and make them accept his return. However, after preliminary battles, Bonaparte could not defeat a pan-European force under Wellington at Waterloo, and with his final taking less than 100 days, he abdicated on June 25th, 1815, fled to the British and was exiled much further away than before. Now on the tiny rock that was St. Helena, he died within six years, on May 5th, 1821, aged 51. No one is really sure how he died.

Historians are divided and publishers are profitable: was he a brutal tyrant or an enlightened despot? A tortured genius or a blunderer who ran out of luck? Given the range of languages the source material of the Napoleonic Wars is spread across, we're unlikely to stop that debate. Yet he remains so interesting because of these contradictions. He was a very good general, if not the best. He was a superb politician, if not the greatest of his era. His legislative contributions weren't perfect but they were massively important. The genius of Napoleon was that he combined talents which would normally be spread among separate people. Bismarck needed Moltke the Elder. Napoleon didn't.

Made in the USA
Las Vegas, NV
26 February 2021